For convenience, the masculine gender has been used in its literary form when referring to God and the human being.

Introduction

How many of us have truly known the quest and search for our spiritual selves? At different times we each may give credence and acknowledgment to some sort of search; and we occasionally speak of awakenings, momentary revelations, uplifted and heightened religious experiences. But how many of us have actually set upon the path to the inward journey, abandoning all exterior and material demands—all friends and family—all ambition—all self aggrandizement—all acquisition—all public approval—for one single goal: the discovery of one's own soul and the expression of the heart's desire.

Avideh Shashaani demonstrates in this book the first evidence I've seen. This is a deeply personal account, and a step-by-step process in seeking God, and in joining the discipleship of a creed... losing the ego and the daily self to find something far more important... the timeless and transcendent eternal "I."

But first our author had to feel a desire beyond all other impulses—beyond tranquility, beyond beauty, beyond knowledge. Her desire would be so overwhelming that it seems the pilgrim's heart would break open with agony and despair. There would be no escaping sorrow, at first, because every atom in Avideh cried for completion. No amount of distraction or comfort could substitute for the enlightenment sought—the total absorption by an accepting God—within herself.

The story is of her love and she has written her heart on the page without shame, without self consciousness, so the world could see, and share the Sufi experience which we discover is lived, not told.

We start our story with Avideh's recognition of herself in a universe which cannot notice her. She likens herself to the tiniest insect ever bred. How could such an infinitesimal creature dare to hope for enlightenment, for eternity, for the timeless light of true and endless love. Through providence she meets individuals studying with the Sufi

Islamic Master Hazrat Pir, Molana-al-Moazam Salaheddin Ali Nader Shah Angha, known to his intimates as Agha Jan. From the moment of initiation into the disciple's world, Avideh was to know every emotion a human being could express, every thought a devoted follower could muster... all, which opened to embrace the intuitive and spiritual knowledge which emanated from Agha Jan, the adored Master of Sufi seekers and practitioners. This book is its disclosure.

Agha Jan's lessons comprise the main substance of the text. His teachings which embody all subject areas use the principles of logic, science, even physics and medicine, to illuminate the higher order of life without death. The beauty of this book is that those of us who don't have direct access to Agha Jan now have the benefits of his thought, and the fruit of his lessons. It is a privilege to read the wisdom and elucidation which Avideh experiences and transcribes for us—transforming the actual and the immediate to a more spiritual world. It is no wonder that there are few volumes of information describing Sufi piety. There is no recipe book or bible available as is found for other world religions. Most bodies of religious thought begin in dogma and end in a monolith of commands and commandments. The belief and the truth of Sufism is in the reality of the heart's journey. To follow the Sufi path is to become an infant learning how to crawl and walk without a tablet of stone, and without blueprints or directions.

This is the mystery we see 'unveiled,' a religion without "How To" books. The Sufi truth is a fragile, evanescent, self-expressed fountain of divine power. We live through this evolution and arrival with Avideh. Her tears are on the page, her supplications, self doubts, personal longings. Finally, as a door opens, we are allowed to enter with her. We don't go as bystanders but companions who are let in to see the rivers she writes of. These carry her jewels, fruits and flowers—a kind of paradise—an ecstasy and magnificence finally found.

We are given many serious messages in *Promised Paradise: Agha Jan–Sufism's Secret Divulged*, and once told we won't forget them. For here is a writing where nothing is held back. Those of us who trust language and spend our lives with it consider words a process toward effect. Avideh plans nothing, manipulates nothing—structures only the truth of utterance, prayer, song, chant, letter, dialogue and poem. It is as if she becomes pure liquid to take a shape in words, within the line, without artifice or design, achieving a symmetry of the highest order, forming an unending song which stays long after the last page is closed.

What is its effect? How does it work on us who are carefully following Avideh on the path of her 'Secret Divulged?' I have never read a work like this which had a physical effect on my body and mind. I pick up the book and I immediately feel the safety of being somewhere I belonged. There is a serenity, absorption, sense of peace and totality which comes with the reading. It's not easy to explain but it's a fact supported by other readers who agree. The genuine world which the book creates is one which we enter. It's a holy state of spiritual order which connects to something within our own being.

One important addition I make is that Avideh is a woman of many facets. One is humor. All that's human and genuine belongs to the Sufi; and laughter is one source of energy. It's as much a part of her depth as her tears... and together they source her self-realization. We find our Avideh is a teacher and a trickster and a saint and an elf rolled in one. Avideh is the East Coast Representative of M.T.O. Shahmaghsoudi (School of Islamic Sufism.) Avideh's international concerns are reflected in the organizations she serves. She is Chairperson of the Board of Directors for Refugee Women in Development. As East Coast Managing Director of Wayfinders, a wellness consulting firm, she is able to impart her own methodologies and philosophies of wellness to the general public. She is the Vice President of the Literary Friends of the D.C. Public Library. She lectures nationally and internationally on Sufism. Avideh is no empress in robes in a marble temple... more an uncontained essence like spirit itself. Out of the jar, free.

I love Avideh's emergence to her reality under the presence and guidance of Agha Jan. *Promised Paradise* is a mystery story, and a magical tale, an adventure story; it's a story not heard before. This book holds the wisdom of prophets and the innocence of the newborn. *Promised Paradise* unveils the Sufi soul, and through this we find our own connection.

Becoming close to God is bringing the qualities God has into oneself. What this means to those of us who are average people—trying to survive, seeking to overcome small daily challenges—is that we learn to live.

Avideh Shashaani has embarked upon a journey to find her personal destiny. If mysticism is the study of life, this book details her life's study. The poet Robert Frost called "passionate preferences" the images we choose to bring into the mind, conscious ideas we nourish, our most rarified thoughts kept alive. In reading Avideh's story, we see one way we are closer to God is through these images of 'passionate preferences' she gives us.

The reason we begin reading *Promised Paradise* is because it's a beautiful story. The reason we finish is because we find the story also belongs to us.

I am grateful, as you will be, to be present at the telling.

Grace Cavalieri
February 4, 1993

Grace Cavalieri is a poet and playwright. She is the author of six books of poetry, the most recent is Trenton (Belle Mead Press, 1990.) She has hosted and produced the long standing program "The Poet and the Poem" on WPFW-FM in Washington, D.C. since 1977. The series has enjoyed national distribution and has recently published an anthology of its poets featured from Grace's public radio program (The Bunny and the Crocodile Press, 1992.) Among many other awards, Grace has won the Pen Syndicated Fiction Prize. She has also recently received an inaugural writing fellowship from the state of West Virginia for drama.

Promised Paradise
Agha Jan–Sufism's Secret Divulged

Avideh Shashaani

In the Name of God
Most Gracious, Most Merciful

God! There is no god
But He,—the Living,
The Self-subsisting, Eternal.
No slumber can seize Him
Nor sleep. His are all things
In the heavens and on earth.
Who is there can intercede
In His presence except
As He permitteth? He knoweth
What (appeareth to His creatures
As) Before or After
Or Behind them.
Nor shall they compass
Aught of His knowledge
Except as He willeth.
His Throne doth extend
Over the heavens
And the earth, and He feeleth
No fatigue in guarding
And preserving them
For He is the Most High,
The Supreme (in glory).[1]
Holy Koran, 2:255

---

[1] Quoted from Yusuf Ali's translation of the Holy Koran.

In Your Name,

O' Flower of Flowers who gives life to all the sickly souls who search for Beauty, and life's Essence. We speak of You not knowing who You are. We adore, worship and love You as much as You deem necessary. We know You as much as You allow. Can we ever truly know You?

Promised Paradise
Agha Jan—Sufism's Secret Divulged

If I were to tell you all the
folds that the journey holds...
The journey's thousands of folds...
To unfold each fold
it would take at least
a thousand days and nights
for each fold to be told.

Did you hear about the tiniest creature that
ever lived on the face of this earth?
She was so tiny that no one ever noticed her;
not even God, so she thought.
She had to wear squeaky shoes so she
wouldn't be stepped on.
She said God is All-Seeing, He'll certainly
take notice of me.
So she set out on the road to make herself
known to God, to call on God.
How can an itsy bitsy little creature be of
any use to God, so she thought.

Shall we go to the garden of paradise? Whose loveliness is beyond our sight? Then close your eyes...it's a lovely day, the loveliest day ever to be seen. The breeze is so refreshing it nests the bees to whisper close to the blossoms of Spring...the dew still languishing on the grass so green...the trees caressing the rays delicately reflecting the early dawn... a languishing fragrance penetrates the air. Each and every breath is joyful in its ecstasy. Well, here you are in the midst of this garden of dreams. From far, the flowers are so abundant the rainbow they display. Now from close, so delicate, each one so gently settled in its own place, yet responding to each and every breath that nature prevails. Step close, look closer and closer until its beauty, its freshness your being disarms. How does this flower know to unfold from roots implanted deep within the soil, to unearth itself and deliver its fragrance for the skies to embrace? How is it done? How does this delicate, unseen, undetected fragrance find its way away from the harshness of the earth? Now that you've seen all these flowers, each different, without duplicate...think if you were to create a flower completely unique, not one to be seen like it, how would it be? Just think, you have all possibilities to create and display the flower of your dreams, in this Garden, the promised Garden where every flower is planted, grown and looked after by Agha Jan's loving Hands. Yes, this is the Garden of Paradise, where all 400,000 flowers, not two alike, await dawn for Agha Jan to shower them with light and dispel the darkness of night.

Once upon a time, not long ago—anywhere between a day and eons ago, a child—"I"—a very young child anywhere between one and 101, on a summer's day, an afternoon, went to visit some friends, have tea in their splendid flower garden.

Stepping unto their garden I saw a flower, how radiant its color, bright violet-pink flowers, set against dark luscious green leaves.

A sense of awe, of warmth, a sense of having awakened to life penetrated deep within me, until tears its colors veiled from my eyes. My friend's voice with the offer of tea called me back to reality. Soon ended my visit, but before I left she said, please take this with you; she offered me the flower pot to take.

Beaming with joy I took my flower pot, and carefully placed it in the seat next to me as I drove toward home. Upon arrival, I took it to my favorite spot, the window-sill where my desk overlooks the lush summer trees. I sat behind my desk, my usual spot when at home, and looked with childish joy at its every petal and leaf. It was not long before my eyes took notice of a small creature making its way out of a newly opened bud. An ant it was, a very small ant. I gazed at it as it slowly scanned its whereabouts. A sudden sadness swiftly rushed the moments of joy aside. How could this ant ever go back to its home? It's miles and miles away from where it came. How could it get back on its own? Two solutions quickly passed through my mind—either take it back, or else let it make its new home here. This is where the story of "I" begins, and this is how it unfolds and unfolds...

My questions began. I spent hours and hours wandering and wondering. Suppose this ant was to make its home here, will it remember its true home ever again? Or, after a while when it's made its home here and found new friends, will it assume that it's always been here, not knowing or remembering how it came to be here, and all the events that happened to lead it here? Well my mind certainly didn't cease to rest, pondering these questions over and over again. The ant was just a means to awaken in me a state we both shared.

Days went by, my questions were left unanswered.

While deep in reflection, I heard one day gentle voices at a table nearby speak words that inspired my heart and mind. How do they know so much? I was so absorbed by what they said that I suddenly found myself sitting right next to them, asking who are you? Where do you come from? Please tell me who is Agha Jan of whom you so dearly speak? Well, they looked at each other and then with a gentle smile said,

"Where shall we begin to tell you our tale? Like you, the symbol of a curious child, we wanted to know where we had come from, why, and what was our part in this world so vast. After years of diligent search and research, and bypassing traps set up by devils in disguise, one day we heard of Agha Jan. Intrigued we were by what we had overheard. How could anyone ever know so much, be so perfect? Impossible, we thought! But we decided we'd give ourselves the very last chance. It wouldn't harm us to go to this place...would you like to come with us and find out for yourself?"

They seemed fine enough young men, polished, well-behaved, learned and bright, surely the least that could happen would be..... Having considered all possibilities I went with them. I was intrigued by their knowledge as we walked the path, and the hour passed as a flash. Slowly and very quietly they turned the door knob, taking off their shoes as they entered the House. I followed, obeying all the rules of the House. As I looked up my gaze was stunned. Where am I? And who are they? What's this halo of tranquility that prevails? A classroom never had I seen so, everyone sitting on the floor, disciplined and quiet, each speaking in turn with firmness and eloquence. Their words rooted in a totality, their logic would be admired by Socrates, so very different from dissected ideologies. My brain couldn't quite detect if it were safe to remain, for nothing there resembled anything known to it. But "I" immediately felt safe, everything had a familiarity, the fragrance that permeated everywhere was most intoxicating. I sat at the very last spot, quiet, closing my eyes and listening to the lesson at hand. The lesson concerned the very last words on what science knows, on how the story of life unfolds.

My story merely begins here; this was my first encounter. I went to each and every class thereafter, many in number. Every discipline was covered. One day as I was leaving class, I thought, well where have I been all this time? As I reflected on the days I had spent there I saw that knowledge, kindness, fellowship, true human values were imparted. Love's the law—the ruled and the ruler of the house. Every child with love obeyed the law, for they knew that wherever they'd be, they'd never be out of Agha Jan's sight. Their only care was to please, and to be loved by Agha Jan. So they studied hard, excelled in the sciences and arts, but above all, they kept their hearts intact for Agha Jan. Much I learned during this time. All children, young and old from all walks of life, counted their days one by one with the hope of Agha Jan's visit to enclose all their days into one. Agha Jan's visit was always a surprise! But, was I to be Agha Jan's child? "You've seen and learned well the rules of the House, but there's one last thing which you must do before Agha Jan comes." I looked up and saw a bright-eyed child.

Days and nights in contemplation I spent, how could I ever create a flower unique? Turmoil and strife slowly crept upon me. I feared failing the test. Alas! Agha Jan was to arrive. Joy and sadness, side by side. If only I had my flower everything would be fine. Hustle and bustle—but all in tranquility and order—day and night. Each child was at the peak of joy and yet so self-contained. Would I see Agha Jan?

A veil of penetrating stillness, that fragrance engulfed the House. The bright-eyed child asked, where's your flower? Agha Jan's arrived. As I turned to leave, my eyes were drawn to the most magnificent... Show me your flower, His gentle voice said. I stood still, and butterflies began fluttering in my heart. This flower I offer to Agha Jan. In darkness its roots toiled—the years before I heard Your name Agha Jan; its stem sprouted—the days I've spent in Your House; its leaves bloomed—the days of anticipation in seeing You; and the petals—the tears of sadness that I may not see You, Agha Jan. As You see, my flower's incomplete, its fragrance You must bequeath, Agha Jan. A flower without Your Breath cannot the skies ascend, Agha Jan. All this I said with floods of tears. I couldn't take my eyes away...it seemed I'd always known Agha Jan.

How can I be left without the joy of seeing Your Face—Beauty unveiled—where shall my eyes search for such beauty untold? My heart was sad, so very sad, my only wish was to look forever in Agha Jan's Eyes, although I was told it was against the House rules. I found the solution. I remembered He had once said, I am always in the company of those who remember me. This was His promise. As this thought passed my mind, I saw Agha Jan's Eyes penetrate mine with a gentle smile. Agha Jan, You unveiled Your Eyes, and through them You opened the galaxies and showed me the stars. It was a journey unknown to the human mind, Agha Jan. Those joyous hours wrapped in your presence, Agha Jan.

Your children are bright-eyed, brisk and young...though their hair be sprinkled white with age, or their back's bent...but agile are they at the call of Your Name, Agha Jan. As all children not knowing what's wrong, they stop to play, their appetite goes, their studies fail, pale they become...because they miss You, Agha Jan. But as soon as signs of earthiness appears in them, you quickly sent that Breath...then each one...each flower in that eternal Garden beams again with life...for they know it's Your love coming to them, and You're at their side.

The story is simple, Agha Jan doesn't believe in keeping His children at His side. Not that I blame You, Agha Jan! He wants them to be independent, shrewd, wise, learned, in other words, He trains them and gives them whatever they need. A mirror reflects what faces it. Agha Jan doesn't believe in the monastic life for His children. He always says, be with others, but don't partake of their bad habits. Agha Jan believes in the tradition of His Holy ancestry, as the Holy Prophet has said, people are like stones whose rough edges are smoothed out by rubbing against each other when washed ashore; it's living among others that brings out the rough edges which must be smoothed out. The more they interact the smoother they become. Agha Jan watches over His children day and night, so they don't stray and drown. No matter how the children grieve, but to them He listens not. Some say, Agha Jan doesn't love us, or else He'd keep us at His side. Others think they're not worthy enough. There's hardly time for another such thought, that through some unforeseen event, they receive their message from Agha Jan. Assured they rest, for Agha Jan knows whatever goes through their hearts.

Agha Jan teaches them the tricks of flight, how to fly and fly and fly. Yes, Agha Jan knows ever so much. I watch Him, mesmerized. He answers each and every question—child and scholar alike—His answers are always so unpredictable. They seem simple, but there's no way its voltage can be adapted for the human brain to comprehend. After some time, when reflection sets in, the meanings begin to unveil and unfold like a beautiful rose, until its essence quenches the thirsty mind and soul. Of course, this is all done with Agha Jan's own Hands.

What pleases Agha Jan is for each child to learn more and more. He is the Law, and Law accepts nothing but perfection. Law gives life, what exists manifests the knowledge it has without any interference. Law accepts nothing but knowledge, for law is Knowledge, just like water submitted to the knowledge it manifests. How does anything know to evolve into what it is? Have you ever seen water say I created water? I made the oxygen and hydrogen combine to become water? Water is water—knowledge manifest. Who is it that directs the process? Agha Jan, You said, knowledge directs, it's silent and undetected, what you see manifest is knowledge unfolded.

Agha Jan's only concern is for each child to manifest the knowledge it has within...wisdom, purity, justice, honor, humility, compassion, kindness, and above all that eternal bond, Love. All this Agha Jan imparts. For knowledge returns to Knowledge. This is the law as said in the Holy Book, "Everything returns to its Origin."

Agha Jan, Agha Jan—my Treasure—the hidden Treasure kept from strangers' eyes. The Treasure the mountains and heavens cannot contain...how can they, for they cannot behold You. How can they love You if they cannot see You? How can those living in deep dark caves be blinded by the sun? Agha Jan, from the tiniest particle in our body, to the stars and galaxies, all are submitted to You, but they don't have a heart to behold and love You. Agha Jan, Your Voice is heard and Your Face is seen in hearts free of arrogance and pride.

Agha Jan, I remember reading the "Verse of Light." I was quite curious to learn how to decode it so I would know its true meaning.

I read so diligently all the books, so many volumes. I studied the works very hard, thinking the meaning would be there, but of no avail. Now before me You stand, "Light upon Light," Agha Jan. After all, the Holy Book is for believers only. And who are the believers, but those to whom You have revealed Yourself. So, for those who begin their journey after the revelation—the toddlers—You are the star in their hearts, to those who've reached maturity, You're the moon in their hearts, and to those who've become ageless, You are the Ever-Eternal Sun. Is this then the meaning of the Holy Verse, "Unto Allah belong the East and the West, and whichever way ye turn, there is Allah's Countenance. Lo! Allah is all-embracing, all-knowing?"

Agha Jan, I recall in a radio interview You explained about a line in Your poem, and You said, "not that I am the sun, but does the sun...." When I first heard You say that, I thought You didn't want to let anyone know who You are. Now, after four years I realize, well, of course, You had to say that, You are not the sun—after all, the sun is but a created power of Your Soul.

Tidings You give to Your children who do all You say, from the a...to... z. You've kept Your word, though in doing all the a...to...z, as a child writing the a,b,c, is very clumsy indeed. I too was quite clumsy, but I persevered, since my intention was quite clear. I wanted to please You...I knew if I learned I would definitely please You, Agha Jan. I know now that the zeal to learn was given by You, so I would move and come closer and closer...to have a chance to learn more and more...to know that I truly don't know...become humble and free...to enter Your House as a newborn child. That thirst to know is so unquenchable that even when my eyes close to rest the thirst continues to prevail. I, thinking that it is my remembrance of You, while it is Your gift of remembrance that calls this hand to move, and this voice to say Your name, Agha Jan. All this is because You don't want the world to absorb me, until I'm completely stable and strong.

Agha Jan, You said, pity, that this body you inhabit you so poorly treat. Your house you look after with more care, simply because you pay for it, and nothing else. Then, You quoted a beautiful verse from Your Beloved Grandfather's book:

Expend fairly, as the occasion calls for
Whatever God has given you, is free.

That was enough to put us to shame. But You didn't stop there. You said, look at every part of your body, the knowledge in every bit of it, no human brain can duplicate. How much are you worth? Just think of how much it would cost to replace just one part? Yet so many parts can't even be duplicated and replaced. This gave us a new perspective as to the value of what we have. You said, think of your body as a beautiful stallion, how would you treat it? You train it with discipline and with care. You don't feed it toxins, exhaust and abuse it. Agha Jan, You said, your body's a vehicle to take you to where you need to go. Make sure you learn how to use it effectively to get to your goal.

Habit, You said, is the dark veil upon knowledge. Knowledge is creative. In action it gives form to that which has not been manifest, thus it is unique. Agha Jan, You said, have you seen two flowers, two birds, two trees, two stones...completely alike? Habit, on the other hand, is mere repetition, regurgitation of what has already taken form; it's so limiting and binding.   Habit is the reinforced states of your sensory experiences.   It's what the brain has gathered through the windows of your senses, then compiled and at best analyzed.

Besides, You said, just suppose you want to repeat every detail of an event, from the surroundings to the words, everything that has shaped that event, can you fully repeat everything? Even if you could, the conditions that have made the event possible no longer prevail; thus, in repeating it you're out of phase with what has made that event possible. So the creativity's lost. Water in drops is less powerful than the brook, the brook less than the river, the river less than the ocean. Knowledge pure is infinite, boundless in power, it pushes everything else aside. Nothing stands in its way. What can stand in front of a turbulent sea, an overflowing dam? Knowledge within you, if not by habit ruled, is creative, for it only manifests that which it truly is. Habit is a sharp sword of destruction, it's a thick veil of darkness over the knowledge you have. But once knowledge is on the rise, habit has no chance to survive. But before it does, the ground must be cleared and prepared for the strong unswerving force to take over. Agha Jan, power is but a speck of dust in Your presence, riches have no value next to Your generous Hands.

You put hell fire before me Agha Jan, so that I may experience what nature and environment have engraved deep within me. You walk me through it day and night, so I become purified. This is Your science, alchemy, turning base metals into silver or gold. Some call it the philosopher's stone, because they know not that it's Your Breath that purifies and turns all within and without into gold. You said, to build, you r st first destroy. The imprint of the past is erased from the pages of the self, habit is uprooted for knowledge to prevail, in other words, the me that was, as "I" to You returns. For You've said, "By Me you shall see, by Me you shall hold, by Me you shall walk, by Me you shall..." So through You all prevails in all. Is this then the meaning of the Holy Verse, "He is God, the One and Only, God, the eternal, Absolute...?"

The passage of time has ceased, its steps are no longer heard. Love has bounded all that was, is, and will be, into one evolving, expanding circle. Its beginning and end is only imagined by those who've not beheld Your fair Face from behind nature's veil, Agha Jan.

In Agha Jan's School each word has a precise meaning, naked without the garment of ignorance and the decay of time. What is sin, someone asked? To die and not realize the truth, which is your right, Agha Jan replied. God's words are only directed to those who search to know the truth. So, sin, angels, heaven and hell are other than people imagine in the confines of their minds. It's meaningless for those not enrolled in God's class.

You ask, what is an angel? Angels are the hidden powers of the soul, Agha Jan responded. Once they are set to work, they, like a magnet, attract all powers within you that are daily dissipated through ill use. As these powers find their direction home, whatever they do, like angels, they are always at God's command. What is the soul, but God's own breath imparted to whomever He likes, when He likes. The seers of the Vedas, Buddha, Moses, Jesus, Mohammad, all 124,000 Prophets (peace and blessings upon them all,) each gave a message suitable for the people of their time. The examples they gave were those the people could relate to. Now people interpret them as they like, without knowing the reality they portray, and think the Prophets' words are outdated. So the message is one: Know yourself, the greatest, highest place is granted to the sons of Man. So what is your choice, to spend all your gifts in the pursuit of your physical life from which you're bound to part? Or your Truth, that which is eternal, everlasting beyond the limitations of earthly life? The important point to know in all this is: Seek the Prophet of your time, so He can purify you and guide you to the fountain of eternal life.

Agha Jan, once You said, man is the architect of his environment, he shapes and forms everything according to the knowledge available to him. His actions are based on his knowledge. The house upon its foundation stands. Your house manifests the knowledge you have. Hell and heaven are created by man's own hands. Anger, greed, envy, jealousy are the fuel for man's hell. Knowledge, the truth of "I"—from which tranquility's gained—is man's heaven on earth. God's words are not intended to bring discomfort, hardship upon mankind, but to show humans how to lay the foundations of their house right, so it lasts. Through ignorance, humans interpreted God's words according to their limited experience, and gave them all kinds of shape and form, like an elaborate house without a foundation for its support.

Agha Jan, do You remember in my first encounter, You lifted the veil from Your Eyes, I traveled through the galaxies and then I saw all the Prophets and all converged into one light, and that one Light was You. Agha Jan, I remember reading the following in one of Your Holy Books, "Observance of eight qualities from eight Prophets are necessary on the journey for the seeker so that he attains firmness of step and returns to his origin: solitude and seclusion from Adam, remembrance from Moses, endurance from Idries, abstention from the senses from Abraham, union of heart from Joseph, silence from Zacharias, fasting from Jesus, and patience and contentment from Ayub." Agha Jan, will You teach me all these, and the other qualities inherent in You?

I remember once You asked, who among you who wears the human skin with all its markings is ready to attest what human attributes and values you portray? You said, I'm not talking of what animals, insects, and plants are capable of doing. Don't forget the sons of Man should reflect what befits their name.

Agha Jan, You said pride, arrogance, prejudice, are all signs of ignorance, the true human rank is beyond these cares. That which we call "man" is created free, naked of all earthly veils. So, the whole intention is for that Jewel to shine through all the 70,000 earthly veils. Of course, this is that everlasting knowledge, that which You impart to whomever You want—that boundless Treasure, Your ordained inheritance of 1,400 years. You never give the slightest hint of all the knowledge You possess. My shame's immense when I remember... thinking You didn't know my state. How could I be in need when the very source of all that is, is with me every instant of every day and night? Can anyone ever know how much You know? Of course it's impossible, Agha Jan.

To figure out what Agha Jan has in mind, when He talks, frowns, or smiles is simply useless. How can the brain of a tiny ant detect the pulse of the universe? One thing is for sure, and that is, wherever Agha Jan's child may be, Agha Jan keeps a close watch over him. Though it may manifest differently...punishment, fear, joy, exhilaration, it's all the training this unruly "self" needs. He crushes in order to build, so the "self" we've come to call "I," may through nature's cloak unveil the true "I." Agha Jan, You once said, no matter how diligently you study— every conceivable book and subject—no matter how many hours you may spend on induction, deduction, discussion, speculation, or infer-ence, through none of them will the truth of "*I*" be known to you. You must be faced with the reality of "*I*" to know "*I*." Just as time unveils the events it holds, so being faced with the constant stable "*I*," your reality will be reflected as a clear mirror before your eyes. Agha Jan, Your Beloved Father has said in His Holy Book, "Part of the truth cannot be known unless through the truth itself." Agha Jan, whenever I say these words to someone, no matter how bright—unless their hearts have been opened by You—they stumble over them. I suppose these words are so well voltaged that they immediately disarm the brain.

What is the measure for gold? What is the measure for truth? What is the measure for love? Can you recognize gold if you haven't seen gold? Can you know truth if you don't know what truth is? Can you know what love is if you haven't experienced it?

Agha Jan, sometimes the moon is small, sometimes it's large, sometimes it's full, sometimes it's new. But no matter if it's night or day, no matter how it looks, I love the moon because it's a reflection of You.

Agha Jan, one thing is for sure, words written to You, if sincere, are accepted for sure. The important thing is to open our hearts to You, Lord of the hearts. Sometime ago in sorrow and remorse I wept, longing for the purity I'd known, wondering what had happened to that innocence. The veils now drawn before "*I*," will they ever be lifted? How I wish I could break through this shell and emerge pure and untouched. In the deep corner of my heart I spoke with You, I am forlorn, Agha Jan. You know everything that goes on within me, I speak with You constantly, please help me. I heard Your voice telling me, you are free. Slowly the chains of boundaries began to break, and the pain of containment began to be relieved.

Agha Jan, Agha Jan, at this half hour past midnight there is nothing that veils You from my heart, Your heart, Your abode. What tranquility and expansion. My heart unfolds every reality behind everything I see. What You've done is beyond belief. I, Your child, how could I dare touch Your innocent child. Your child, Your truth, Your everlasting grace and beauty. Perhaps this is the stage as stated by Your Beloved Father as "the mount of affection of the heart." I experience the affection that comes from You in everything that I touch. My enemy within You've conquered with love and knowledge. Agha Jan, Agha Jan, Monday eve, You gave me Your blessings complete. I keep and cherish them and declare them loud and clear. I say to everyone, come to the House of Love, everyone's welcome to this abundance. Come empty and receive your share of this everlasting Grace. O! Agha Jan, Your child is breaking through the womb of adolescence towards maturity to become the ripened fruit from the tree so well cared for, and tended to by Your gracious Hands, in the Garden of Paradise.

Agha Jan, for a long time I pondered as to how these sweet melodies of love are strung together so exquisitely by the most eminent Masters. Would it ever be possible to experience the same? What gift, what blessing it would be. Just today, You gave me a glimpse, a taste of that luscious exquisite flavor of love. Each step away from others lifts a veil of separation between You and "I." How can the flavor of a food be known by just tasting one of its ingredients? So, love too is only known when all the veils are lifted, and only Love remains. That's what You said, Agha Jan. Agha Jan, Agha Jan, You are love, total love, Agha Jan.

Worship changes form, until object and subject become ultimately one, from separation into unity; then, as one, in absolute rapture, they evolve. So worship is not an act of duty, penance, but it's an enraptured, expanding dance of love. This, then, is the meaning of true worship that Your Breath bestows. I recall reading in one of Your Beloved Father's Books, that the word for love in Arabic is *ishq*, derived from *ashaq*, which means bindweed. This is a plant of more or less twining habit and tends to interlace with plants among which it grows. First it turns red, then yellow, then disperses and is ultimately annihilated. Agha Jan, You've always said that states in the physical world have a spiritual counterpart. We must be the bindweed that nourish from You—the genuine Essence—and must go through all the stages, until we're annihilated in

You. How else can we be one with You. Our boundaries must drop for Love to remain.

Agha Jan, You've also explained to us that love manifests in different forms, but it comes from a main source which resides in the heart. You said, starting at the very base, there's the love that takes on physical forms, then there's the love of the mother and child, then there's the love of the student and Teacher, and at the summit is the love for God. Agha Jan, You never leave anything out! Agha Jan, I can say I've experienced it all, except the love of mother and child, and ever since knowing You, You've been my Mother, Father, Friend, Teacher, and God. I simply don't need anyone anymore.

Agha Jan sends His children—His own reflected images, that is, those who've learned well the art of love—to go and find those children who're searching for Father's loving call.

Yes, Agha Jan shows His children His dominions, but a little at a time. One must be ready, one must be prepared, be steadfast and patient in all the trying and the joyful times. Agha Jan never lets you think you've completed your learning. He says if you become proud of what you know, then you stop learning. So, He teaches His children the subtle arts: humility, endurance, compassion, self-worth, gentleness, selflessness...all human attributes, all the words one reads in books that seem only saints of long ago possessed. They are but a drop of all that Agha Jan owns.

Agha Jan wants His children to display the perfection that befits their name. The sons of Man, the animal state must put behind. Honor, chivalry, charity, compassion, tenderness, generosity, are the least they own from the treasure chest Agha Jan bestows. His children are trained to guard over the unruly "self." Love is the ammunition with which this battle is won.

Agha Jan, once You said, a jealous person is like a child with an ice cream cone in hand. Seeing another child with an ice cream cone, he throws his own to the ground and runs after the other. All that he has left is a melting ice cream cone on the ground!

One of Agha Jan's children, who is a clear image of the love Agha Jan bestows, said to me, you know the minute Agha Jan set His Eyes on you, you were born anew, because that encounter in heaven took place. Your recognition of His true identity, your knowledge of Him, in primordial time took place, long before your earthly shell which nature took billions of years to mold. A long journey you've made, but your earthly form slowly made you forget your true place, so it took a little tiny ant to let you know the earth's not where your true home is. Agha Jan's Hand, although not seen at that time, led you every step until your meeting took place. His children are dear to Him, of His own Essence they are. How can He let His children stray, be lost, forlorn, without guardian, without Father's love, in this world for long? But that separation is a lesson Agha Jan's children must learn, as He says, "Thirst seek, not water." Patient is He and watchful, until every single child comes home to Agha Jan.

Agha Jan, a thought occurred to me, how silly of Your children to look through Your books and try to understand Your words. How funny, how can we know what You say? Your experience of the universe is from a 360 degree angle. Well, You are patient Agha Jan. You teach us to experience the a,b,c of the knowledge each word's endowed with. Then the unfolding starts to take place. All is in Your Hands, Agha Jan. You want to teach the laws of the universe, but You want a bright student, eager, driven with love, so all that You know to him You'll impart. The very best of us can be compared to a toddler placed in Einstein's super advanced physics class.

The journey which brought me to see You, Agha Jan, is known as the Holy Pilgrimage. In a single glance You swiftly brushed all the dust away, and there I stood, a newborn child. The freshness of Spring, the joy of youth, the playfulness and innocence of a child with that one glance You bestowed upon me. A young bud, ready to absorb all the breath of Dawn. This abundance, I must keep sacred, intact. Now the guidance and Guide within my heart reside. Agha Jan, Agha Jan, You are always present, Agha Jan.

Agha Jan, Agha Jan. I can't stop saying Agha Jan.

I heard all your children—all 400,000 of them—in one voice say, Agha Jan, Agha Jan. What lovely chorus. I long for the chorus to get louder and louder so I can hear your name, Agha Jan. I'll say Your name to everyone, Agha Jan. The more children there'll be, the more I'll hear Your name, Agha Jan. I can't be blamed, You've planted the love, taught me to love, Agha Jan, Agha Jan.

Agha Jan, to have been in Your presence for 11 days, from morning to night, I thought I must have done something right. But what a childish fancy, trying to calculate what may please You. Does love have an accountant at hand? You do as You wish. So, calculation too You've taken away from me—what a relief—to bring me closer and closer to You, so that Love's will penetrates closer and deeper. Love's Your agent, the mightiest, wisest, most efficient of Your angels, Agha Jan— God in nature manifest.

Agha Jan, I've closed my ears, my eyes, my heart to all else but You. I don't want to hear any but You, Agha Jan. You've closed all the channels that lead me astray, so that none other but You shall be seen or heard. The pit of my stomach is uneasy, afraid that all this ecstasy may wilt and pass away. My head says hurry, reap the harvest while the abundance is at hand. But, then I listen to my heart, the place where I know You abide. Agha Jan, it tells me and assures me that if at every instant I call You, You are with me. You are with me no matter what, Agha Jan. It's me, this neglectful, playful child that forgets Your guiding Hand. I am assured that if I take every step with Your remembrance Agha Jan, how could I ever fear separation, neglect and error, Agha Jan? How can I fear the world, or need anyone, or turn to anyone but you, Agha Jan?

Agha Jan, those 11 precious days in Your presence, I tried so very hard to absorb Your every word, Your every gesture to understand and memorize. That chapter's closed. For what You've planted and nurtured within me in those 11 days, these senses could not detect. But to "I," the soul, you revealed all there was to know. Revelation upon revelation. Ceaseless are Your skills, You are a marvel, Agha Jan.

Each moment is now as a radiant sun, lighting, illuminating the darkness of every instant. On the way back, Agha Jan, I kept reviewing all that I had learned, fearing that I would forget. You know my memory, Agha Jan! I thought I was so awful, absolutely so base and undeserving of Your attention, that for sure I'd been given the honor of being in Your presence for the very last time. But two very important lessons crept into my mind. You had said, I keep cleaning this pipe everyday, and yet it keeps on bringing taint upon itself, what should I do with this pipe? Agha Jan, I was so ashamed. I thought you must mean us. You keep cleansing us, and yet we keep playing in mud. I said to myself, is this a warning from Agha Jan? I also remembered Your words from the most Exalted Lord of the believers who said, "The past is past, the future's not come, but now is what you have." History You've erased, and in its place You've given me the now, this very creative moment. It's creative because it is in total reliance and remembrance of You. How can it not be creative when it's the Creator that the "now" bestows. All that exists is submitted to this law—to be in the moment, to unfold the knowledge it's been bestowed.

Faith and love are essential for any creative act. Faith, because no trace of doubt must be where reliance on You resides. For You will be the doer, not I, Agha Jan. So my mind, this unique and perfect brain which You've bestowed, its task is to help me survive in the natural world. Its other task is to look and question about the marvels of existence until it's guided to the Truth where its answers are found. In essence, its value lies in providing the steps for that Meeting, that Encounter—for the divine birth to take place.

Agha Jan, I remember one day one of Your children of whom you said such rare high words told us that Your Beloved Father would say to people, "Come in, you're invited to join in the banquet with the King," and people would say, "Thank you, thank you, we enjoy being in the stable, from it we do not want to part." This must seem as quite an insult to the noble ears of proud and rational humans who think they're kings. I always think, why do You bother, Agha Jan? Let them stay in their stables. Stable is the place where animals are kept. Unless we come to know the reality of "Self," we are no different than animals kept in stables. So this body serves as a stable, there's nothing derogatory about a stable, if meant for animals. The body can house the animal self, or the self that's been cleansed and attained the divine state. You said, the ladder starts from the stable and ascends to the Throne of God. Where do you want to be on this ladder?

Agha Jan, humans do see things from their tinted lenses indeed. The frog sees the world differently from us. The world through the lens of the spider, the butterfly, the eagle and mouse, looks different. Should we not look for vision, if we want to escape tunnel vision?

Agha Jan, how does a butterfly see a rose from close? Butterflies are so playful. O' Agha Jan, are they so beautiful and light because they've flown away from the shell that made them crawl on the earth? They must know the meaning of freedom. Did they prepare in the winter days, so they could fly to You when Spring finally came? Is that why the roots of the rose toil so hard, so its fragrance can finally ascend to You, Agha Jan? Agha Jan, my heart stops in awe when You lift the veils of nature from before my eyes. Everything is in constant rapture of You, Agha Jan.

Agha Jan, Your Beloved Father has said, "It is fear and hope that keep the seeker moving on God's path." I thought about this a great deal and realized that's exactly what You do with us. If we did not fear losing You, we wouldn't keep our focus and behave, and if we didn't have hope in Your Generosity and Love, we couldn't go on. Is this correct, Agha Jan? At the end of our services we are always served sweets and tea. One day, the oldest sibling asked us if we knew why this was done? We tried to be clever, but he's so smart. He said, they are symbols—representing the sweetness of the Path and its bitterness. Of course we can all attest to that, Agha Jan.

Agha Jan, Agha Jan, Agha Jan, Your Name brings joy to hearts, Your Name brings comfort to hearts, and awakens dormant hearts, it also brings fear to your children, young and old. You've taught us to be honest and true, at all times, unconditionally. But we never know how You'll respond to our innermost confessions and thoughts. But underneath it all, we know that You love us all, for You are the Gentle, the Loving, the Tender.

I remember once, I said: Agha Jan, people say, how can God speak, how can God hear? I had no answers for them, without divulging the unspeakable truth. You said, ask them, do you see, do you hear, do you speak? They'll say yes. Then say, if you see, hear and speak, where did you get it from? At the end they'll narrow it down and say, Existence. Then tell them, if you have gotten this much from Existence, which is but a drop, then isn't existence All-Seeing, All-Hearing, All-Speaking? Well, Agha Jan, this certainly crushes all challenges from the start.

The tales which I can tell are endless... endless for at least 11 years. It would take me 11 years—day and night—to recount every moment of my experience under Your guiding Hand. That's assuming there it stops. Well, hopefully not. Agha Jan, the Beloved Lord Amir-al-Moemenin said, "Not a moment passes that I do not learn." Agha Jan, how can You learn anything new? You are Knowledge. Well, this mystery still needs to be revealed to me. But could it be that my limited perception sees everything as having a beginning and end? I recall that Your Beloved Father said 35 years ago in *The Epic of Existence*, "The universe is evolving too!" So, You are the Center, Agha Jan.

Agha Jan, Agha Jan, Agha Jan, my tales of enrapturement are a million fold. One fold would take at least a thousand days and nights to recount. That's how You break the boundaries of time. A thousand years becomes but a fleeting instant in the galaxies of time. We had been told that every single gesture of Yours has a significance, a prayer, a meaning, a healing, while outwardly it may be just smoking a pipe, cleaning it, stirring Your tea, offering food to someone from Your plate. For You don't do anything in jest. We'd take all this information to our laboratories for analysis. Well of course it's funny. How can our limited

experiences unfold the grand play of Your magic? I guess our percep-
tions are like ants peeking through beads, thinking they're seeing the
universe through high-powered telescopes. But Agha Jan, we are elves
and we can never know the Majesty of Your works. Is this the meaning
of the Holy verse, "God's ways are mysterious, human beings can
never know them." But I suppose after we are purified and attain our
true human state then the mysteries do unfold.

Agha Jan, when the air is crisp everything seems cheerful and clear,
when it's hazy, we have no energy or joy. Agha Jan, does the same hold
true for the states we move through to reach You? I know one day my
heart's fueled with love, another with calm, another with longing,
another with sadness, another with passion...no two days have been
alike since I've seen You, Agha Jan. How can they be? The days that
You're close, and the days that You seem far and the days in between,
all bring tidings of You. Agha Jan, is this the meaning of the Holy Verse,
"The heart of the believer is between the two fingers of God, He turns
it whichever way He wants."

Agha Jan, I know what I write will be blasphemy to so many. But I
don't care, I'm free. I know so much, that even if I'm cut to pieces each
speck of my being will call Your name, Agha Jan. They don't know,
Agha Jan.

Agha Jan, I was just thinking about all Your children, all 400,000 of
them, running back to their homes at midnight and saying the Holy
Verse for 12 minutes while watching the luminous lamp. I guess you
don't have a moment's rest, never sleep. That's what the Holy Verse
says, "God! There is no god but He—the Living, the Self-subsisting,
Eternal. No slumber can seize Him nor sleep...." Well, all these 400,000
children in all parts of the world on different time zones running to You,
calling You in every manner possible. Well, it's understandable. You
are the Father and responsible for every bit of our lives, that is, if we
behave. But You have renegades like me, who are never satisfied with
whatever attention You give to them. We keep calling and calling,

asking for more. No wonder, Agha Jan, Your Ears hurt so. It's not only our own laments we bring to You, but You're so generous, You look after our friends and family, their friends and their families. Agha Jan, one of the older siblings told me in confidence that You read 4,000 letters each night. So, who's left in the wide, wide world to whom You do not tend? They don't even know it's You who bestows upon them such grace. They think it's the imaginary God to whom they pray, the one sitting on the clouds with the white beard. To the Christians, He's the father; to the Jews He's the light on Mt. Sinai; and the Moslems—here I simply give up! Never ever has God's name been so badly abused. But how can I divulge the truth, and tell them that Your beard's not white?

Forgiveness, forgiveness, the truth must not be divulged! Agha Jan, Agha Jan, it's only You who knows how I searched and searched until I found You, my Home, my Friend, my Father, my God. I looked under every word. I did what all the teachers said. I fasted, I prayed. I thought I knew how to meditate. I read the Holy Books. But my heart was never satisfied, it remained locked. My heart knew what my brain knew not. So when my eyes saw You, my heart confirmed that my search had at long last reached its end. What could be left when one has seen the Face of God?

My eyes search the horizon, at the point where the sky and earth meet by the glow of the last rays of dusk, hoping that I may see Your Eyes, again and again, Agha Jan.

Agha Jan, I remember I asked You what to say to people who think they know God by reading the Holy Books. You said, tell them, if reading books about love gives you the same experience as being in love, then reading the Holy Books will give you the experience of knowing God! Agha Jan, one other time I came to You and asked, what do I tell people who think they know God, just because they've heard about God? You said, tell them, is your hunger satisfied if I eat when you're hungry? You get up and reach for food. Why do you think by listening to others you know God? Agha Jan, once I asked You, what do I tell people who think they're Moslems, Christians, or Jews, etc., just because they were born into it? You said, tell them, does it satisfy you if your parents were in love, or do you want to fall in love and have the experience yourself?

Agha Jan, I remember once someone came to You and said he wanted to become a Moslem. You looked at him and said, what has Jesus done wrong that you want to follow Mohammad? You said, if you knew the reality of Jesus, you would know that religion doesn't depend on a name. So often after Your lectures people come up to You and say we want to change and become Moslems, and You say, "I teach stability, not change!"

Agha Jan, everything looks different when it's far, than when it's close. When the plane goes up very high, the clouds beneath seem like white sheep, the houses look so tiny and humans cannot be seen. How does the universe look through Your infinite sight, Agha Jan? Agha Jan, whenever we're before You, it appears that You are still. Will we ever know Your speed? I suppose traveling beyond the speed of light must seem still. But, I think the answer is, how can You possibly need to travel, when You are everywhere!

Agha Jan, I recall an example Your Beloved Father has given in explaining the state of revelation. He has said people think that when they read the Holy Book they can understand it with their brain cells. The Holy Book wasn't revealed to the Prophet through brain cells. Revelation is this, "Suppose I'm sitting in a large house, and I can expand to the extent of the house, now do I need to get up and go over and open the door? Revelation is a state of spiritual expansion, when the soul is no longer confined to the body, but has attained oneness with God. In other words, the speaker is now God!" Agha Jan, this is why the Prophet of Time must be revealed through our hearts by God.

Agha Jan, Agha Jan, Agha Jan. Here I go again. Whatever happened to self-discipline? When it comes to Your Name, discipline simply vanishes. I can sit for days on end...forever saying Your Name, Agha Jan. Is this what is called remembrance? In the Holy Book it is said, "For without doubt in the remembrance of God do hearts find satisfaction."

I also hear Your voice, soothing and penetrating. Just the other day when I was waiting for instructions, I heard You speak to someone in English. There ended my attention to hear the instructions. I must have squeezed myself through the lines and absorbed every single vibration of Your voice. Thereafter, for days I was in orbit again.

Agha Jan, it's been sometime now that You speak through a veil. The instructions come through someone else, but I can hear You regardless. I hear You when You lift Your brows, or motion with Your Eyes or Hands, and above all I can feel Your Breath reach and penetrate my heart.

Agha Jan, I've often wondered why You don't unveil Yourself to everyone. But how can anything ever get done, if all everyone wanted to do was to be by Your side and to love You? When I listen to the sky and the galaxies at the hours past midnight, I hear the echo of Your Name, Agha Jan. Where is it in the universe that pulsates not with Your Name, Agha Jan?

Agha Jan, I used to be deadly threatened if You gave more attention to anyone else. But I was a toddler then, thinking that Your love was limited, like humans. But why is it that my thirst is never quenched, the more You give the more I want. I know in the Holy Book You have said, "Natural appetite is insatiable," but You didn't say that the desire for God's love is the same. Is it because the desire's given by God when He wants to release His child from the natural appetites? Well, Agha Jan, I think I'm learning a lot. But You never tell us if we've passed our tests and moved up a grade. You once said, never have your eyes set on how far you can get, the secret is to have your eyes fixed on the Face of God.

I can only sigh, there's five long days left before I can gaze at Your beauteous Face, Agha Jan. Just to absorb Your every single gesture. The only time I never dare lift up my eyes to behold You is at meals. I know that's truly rude. But I must confess once or twice, I've peeked, and You've been generous not to scold me. What torture to have to look at my plate, when my heart's desire is to look at Your Face.

Agha Jan, I've come to the understanding that scholars of Sufism don't really know what Sufism's about. If they did, they'd all be lined up at Your door. For God's been the way and the goal for those whose works are revered by scholars throughout the world. Don't they see that to know the reality of what Sufis have said, they too must be faced with the Face of God? Agha Jan, is it true that scholars like to have everything dead, otherwise how could they study them?

Agha Jan, Your knowledge precedes time. Even if we calculate, we'll have to go back to Your Holy ancestry, 42 generations, and then to the Holy Prophet, and that's 1,400 years. Now this is the direct line, not counting all the 124,000 Prophets who preceded them. But this is only history—Your manifestation in human form—You are the Eternal.

Once I asked You, why is it that people don't search for the Truth? You said it's always been the same, nothing's changed. It's only to a handful of people in each age to whom God's revealed, and they keep the torch of love aflame, others simply regurgitate. I quickly thought, of all the billions and billions of people in the world, I'm one of the few to whom You've revealed Your Face, Agha Jan. It is Your promise in the Holy Book, "And those who strive in Our (Cause,) We will certainly guide them to Our Paths."

Agha Jan, no one who has not beheld Your Face knows what those who have are speaking of. How can they know what Saint Teresa of Avila said? How do they know to whom she spoke? Can anyone speak so endearingly to a Beloved that one has not seen?

Agha Jan, You said, if you keep asking God to take care of your needs, is He better than a hired hand? You quoted from Your Beloved Father, "A god worshipped for the sake of worldly fulfillment is not great."

What magic! Agha Jan, whenever we, Your children, gather, we just talk and talk about You. We're so foolish, we think You don't hear. And when one of the clever ones speaks up and says, God is always present, and with pride recites the Holy Words, "If two people speak about me, know that I am present." Well, that's enough to put us on our best behavior, and we quickly sit in our meditation pose. How many hours of painful sitting we've endured in preparation for being in Your Presence. It never fails, it doesn't take long before I see that all the practice has been in vain, the pain simply refuses to go away. How to shift without You noticing? Yes, stupid me, thinking that something can cross my mind without You knowing it, let alone very, very slowly shifting my little toe.

But, Agha Jan, do You know what else I've learned from Your words, "If two people speak about me, know that I am present?" The very first time I heard these words, I quickly realized this was the key to being with You all the time. Sometimes I wonder if I speak in my sleep about You, Agha Jan.

Agha Jan, I've been slowly sharing these pearls of wisdom You've bestowed with the toddlers in the class. I can always pick the newly hatched ones from the old. They always have an air of knowing it all about them. It's true they've heard all the wisdom there's to know, but the danger lies when they think they know it too. It's not long before You set them straight, for they're put through the experience. The fluffy feathers fall, and new ones start to grow. How can they fly if their wings don't grow, Agha Jan?

Agha Jan, do You remember how sad I was before I saw You? I remember seeing the Madonna of Seville's face in Spain and I saw my own pain and grief in her bejeweled face. No one must have known such pain. No one must have ever felt so sad. If they had, there would have been a new word invented for it by now. For sadness doesn't even come close to how I felt. Perhaps they died before they had a chance to see Your beauteous Face. Now, Your Presence engulfs my heart, my soul, my being in and out, Agha Jan.

Agha Jan, I love these words, "Eternity is the Face of God."

Agha Jan, You've answered my questions, none is left. The load of not knowing is what causes stress and old age. People try to imitate Christ (peace be upon Him) in order to be good Christians. How can they imitate Him if they haven't seen Him? Are they just imitating their own imaginings? So often, I've been tempted to tell them how they can see Christ, but I know if I should tell them, I'll fall to Your wrath, and I'll be banned from hearing and seeing You for the rest of my life. I guess they'll have to search and search as I did if they're sincere. My lips are sealed, Agha Jan, but how can I control my eyes? Your love pours through them, day and night; even my fingertips burn when I speak of You.

Agha Jan, someone I know said he was an agnostic, and he went to Church. I asked him why? He said, he liked Jesus' honesty of character. I said, if you're an agnostic it means you're not certain that God exists, while Jesus said He was the son of God, He attested to the presence of God. How can you say He was honest, when you don't believe what He said?

Agha Jan, when I go to teach all the skills You've taught me, the other children want to treat me with pomp and fuss. I keep telling them that I'm just like them, our only difference is in the number of days we've been blessed to be in Your Presence, Agha Jan. I'll always be Your child, no matter what age my cells may bear. People count their age by the number of years their cells have been theirs. My age began when You accepted me as Your child, Agha Jan. But isn't it foolish to count one's age according to the cells? Even then, the age would be billions of years according to the genetic age! But does God's Breath have an age? Agha Jan, it's Your inspiration that keeps Your children alive, ageless and young.

Agha Jan, last year You sent me on a trip. You said it's vacation time. My heart just stopped. I didn't want to tear away from all the assignments I so sacredly held. You said, I'd be met at the airport. No more details were given. I knew no one, nor anyone's name. How would I recognize them? So I went through customs, and there a mob stood waiting to greet their dear ones. It took me but a moment to scan the crowd and find the eyes that sparkled with Your love. What better sign can anyone wear? What better way is there to find one's brothers and sisters that one's never seen? Agha Jan, is this similar to the state after death? How will anyone know You in the hereafter, if they haven't beheld Your Face here?

Agha Jan, please don't ever leave us. One of Your older children once told me, be smart, cry and weep, and ask Agha Jan if you can go to see Him, I assure you that's the trick. Well, I certainly learned that wasn't for me. I lost my balance and fell off my star. Just to get back on took a long, long time. Well, now I don't listen to anyone. Each gets his or her instructions directly from You. What works for another may be deadly for me. So, I just go to my heart and ask You for directions. Then, I quickly pour out all my heart's laments. My pleas are answered even before the last word's finished. It's not only me who knows this. It's now common knowledge—Your miracles. I can't even count the numbers that I've seen in these 11 years.

Agha Jan, there are stations and states through which Your children must pass —70,000 veils of light and darkness the Holy Prophet said— before we can reach You. I certainly can vouch for that. I don't think I can count those I've passed through, but I know there are many more to pass through. I must not think of the difficult times, the dry, arid, bitter cold states, where our hearts are blocked from Your love. I've compared notes, when the drought or blizzard hits, it doesn't spare any of us. These are the times we all welcome death. We all say, what's the point of living if we don't have Agha Jan's love? Death is safe haven during such times. But You've also taught us that the common thinking about death is totally wrong. You've said, the state you're in, when nature's shell you discard, is the state you'll be in thereafter. So there's no escape. We know we must endure the cold, harsh winter days. If not, how else can we be cleansed and become purified and shine like mirrors reflecting Agha Jan's light? Patience, patience. Faithful, steadfast patience—to be steadfast through the difficult times so we may always remain at Agha Jan's side.

Agha Jan, some of the siblings who are undergoing for the first time incubation look at me with wondering eyes, with so many questions.

They do not know that purification is a painful process. I look at them knowing that I cannot say much. If I do I would deprive them of their fair share, for they must have the experience. I just say, trust, have faith, everything is as it should be. Don't worry, Agha Jan's watching. I know their pain. How much of all imprinted traits of all the genetic inheritance of thousands of years have you cleansed me of? I suppose the Path is a continuous state of incubation—a laboratory for those entrusted to Your care. We are put through the purifying process, and we are faced with traits we never knew we had. Yes, all of it we have. Only a conducive environment was needed for them to surface... jealousy, pride, greed, envy, and all the other traits every single human being has. Through the assignments, interactions, and all other matters these traits are aired out. And how we hate ourselves when we see our ugliness reflected before our face. But, after each phase we feel the change, the release from the "animal self." How much must we pay for all that's gone before us!

Agha Jan, You once said, for one thought that you have now, five generations after you will have to pay for that thought. God didn't send His Prophets to give you hardship, but to show you a way that would make things for you and for generations after you easier. Whatever you think or do is recorded within you, when you leave this earthly form you will take all of your traits with you. If you're greedy, envious, jealous, etc., that's how you will be in the hereafter as well. If being this way is painful here, know that the pain will remain with you in the hereafter. Since people can't see through a wall, they think nothing exists on the other side of the wall. Ask God to give you vision so you will take heed of what I say.

Agha Jan, people have interpreted the exalted state of "poverty" to mean being lazy, not working, and living on other people's money and toil. They don't know that this is the state of having attained oneness with God. It is the state where no "self" remains and only God remains. Therefore, it is only in this state that one can say, *la-elaha-ella-Allah* (there is no other but God.) So, poverty means true abundance.

Agha Jan, it's no wonder that people have given up looking for You. Those who call themselves Your representatives—Moslems, Christians, Jews, no one's exempt—have set the precondition, the way to You is to go through them. Well, who in his right mind wants to go through them? With all their earthly blisters, one's afraid of getting contaminated and die of ignorance.

If people would be told that they only have to look right in their own hearts to see You, things would be so simple and pure. You've always said people always look elsewhere for what they themselves possess. Such blessed words, Agha Jan!

So Your children don't stray and get hurt, You require of them to check in regularly, and that's the five daily prayers. You make sure they come home each night, so You can tuck them in safely, and that's the midnight vigil—the coming home to Agha Jan. Sometimes pride takes over, and we think we're too old to check in with home. So, the world takes hold and, badly bruised, we return home. You told us one day, don't think you pray for My sake. You pray to maintain your health. Remember, cells don't require prayers in order to be sustained. But there's one prayer that's different than the rest, and that's the midnight prayer, "the prayer gift of love." This you offer on your own without lament or fuss, because it's a prayer of love—that is if you want.

Agha Jan, there's a saying in Persian, "Rushing is the devil's work." So I thought, why has this been said? You've told us many times that so many of these sayings were rooted in the teachings of Your Holy ancestors, but through time they just became commonplace terms, and the message was lost. I thought about this particular term and put it in a mathematical equation, the way You've taught me. I realized that the devil equals cellular instigations. Cellular law asks of them to multiply and multiply and expand. To multiply and expand, they must absorb and expand, and that's survival. So human nature's prone to hoard and devour, therefore it rushes to hoard. Anyone who hoards must come from scarcity. Then I looked at the other side of the equation. The source of life and knowledge is in the heart. The heart is the sanctuary of God, thus the heart takes its command from God. Does God need to rush? God is all-encompassing. So where is it that He is not? So He can't rush. The conclusion is, whoever rushes is not submitted to God. Agha Jan, is this correct?

Agha Jan, there is something that puzzles me. People get fined and punished for drunken driving. The law is to protect the public. But why are commercials that encourage people to drink allowed to be aired? Is it for population control, or a form of conspiracy? I heard that the state controls all liquor sales, and the tax goes to the government for public interest! If I allow myself to think of such things, I'll never get a night's sleep.

Agha Jan, something else that intrigued me was this. I went to a poetry reading where the Poet Laureate was to read. I listened to the glorious introductions, and to his own reading as well. When the audience was allowed to ask questions, I innocently asked him if he was familiar with the writings of the Sufis? He lifted his left eyebrow and looked down at me from the top of his spectacles and said, "Slightly, I'm not interested in spiritual matters." Agha Jan, is this intellectual snobbery, or is it what he really feels? One would think someone in his position would have a deeper understanding of matters relating to the soul. Perhaps, for him poetry is inspired by the cells!

Agha Jan, these words of the Lord of believers simply devastated me. He said, "Truth is not revealed in history. If the historian favors someone, he writes favorably about the situation; if he is an enemy, then he writes disfavorably about it. In neither case will the truth be known, so be the child of your Time."

Agha Jan, once a historian came to you and said he wanted to write a book on the socio-political aspects of Sufism and propose alternatives for Islamic fundamentalism. You looked at him with patience and said, who murdered John F. Kennedy? What about Abraham Lincoln? Suppose their killer was a "Christian;" what does that have to do with Jesus or Christianity? What is involved here is power, other matters are brought into it to convolute the whole issue. Those in power are not

interested in peace. The reason for wars is economics. The Prophets
teach humans to live economically, not to hoard, not to be greedy. It
doesn't mean you should not have sound economic systems; on the
contrary, if humans are taught not to be abusive, sound systems would
survive. Which one of the "Christian" leaders in the world lives like
Christ? Should we say there is something wrong with Christ or His
teachings or, rather, people do not know the reality of what He taught?

You continued, and said, you will never know the truth through
history. Even if everything is written truthfully you will not know its
reality. Truth does not need history. The sciences need history. When
you come to know the truth, it encompasses history. To clarify this point
You added, there are not "religions" but only religion, and Sufism is the
reality of religion. It means you must experience the reality of the
teachings of the Prophets, and not observe rituals blindly! Water is
water, if you've drank it you know what it is and you know what it does,
and no one can persuade you to think differently. Now call it by
different names, each language has its own name for water. Does the
reality of water change because the name changes? So, first know the
truth. When you have a solid foundation, then the rest follows.

Then You paused for a moment looking deeply into his being, and
asked him, do you want to know what religion is? He turned pale and
said, yes. Agha Jan, you put so many questions to him that I thought
he was going to pass out. You said, how many wars in the name of
religion have been fought? How many are being fought? What are they
fighting over? God? How many gods are there? Let's suppose that
Moses, Jesus, and Mohammad (peace be upon them all) lived at the
same time, would they fight each other? What would they be fighting
over? If they are fighting over God, then which one is lying? How will
you know which one is lying? Agha Jan, I can't recall all of Your
questions. There was another pause, and as You looked at him You said,
religion is God. If you know God, you have religion. Otherwise,
whatever you have is a figment of your imagination. Then You said, the
Holy Prophet has said, "Whatever you distinguish with your thought,

no matter how precise and subtle it may be, is a creation of your own thought and not worthy of worship because it is not the truth." You said, who created the Shi'a and the Sunni? Who created all the sects in the Christian faith and so on? Is it God, His Prophets, or human foolishness, greed for power and control, and so forth? God's message as given through His Prophets is very simple: If you know Me, you will know your own truth. Now, is there room for religions, sects, etc.? Just open your eyes and see who is getting the free rides!

Agha Jan, just the other day this woman asked me how You respond to questions, what is Your approach? I said, whatever You say is like a trump card!

Agha Jan, once You told us that the true meaning of the word *Khaneghah* is House of Time. And You've also told us be the child of our Time. I realized when the Prophet of Time is inwardly known to us, then we are His children, and we live in our Time. We do not depend on empty ritual and ceremonies to know the words of God. How else can we know what is expected of us? Agha Jan, You said, true human right is for you to ask God to show you Your Prophet of Time so He can teach you the laws governing your being, so you can live in peace and know your eternity. Agha Jan, we look forward to the days that we can come to the *Khaneghah*, because we know that's where You reside.

Agha Jan, do You remember the time I was so sad—but of course You remember, You remember all things we forget, plus things that have not even happened yet—I wrote You a story that I never mailed, because it was too sad. Here's the story:

Did you hear about the morning glory that never bloomed again?
They say,
there was a morning glory that never ceased to open its bloom
to the very first rays of the rising sun.
The story's told,
that the sun did not shine for our morning glory one day,
nor the next day,

nor the next...
nor the...
Then the sun rose one day again,
but the morning glory did not budge
did not stir,
did not bloom,
not that day,
nor the next...
nor the...
Everyone thought it so strange,
they gathered to see what was amiss,
they gently held one frail petal aside
to find a water pool inside
You see,
our morning glory worshipped the sun,
as soon as the sun would set
the sighs and laments of our morning glory
would form into a tear drop,
but the sun would melt away each tear drop each day
with its loving rays
So, you see when the sun ceased to shine,
our morning glory's laments
gathered and gathered
day after day
until....

So, morning glory, my flower, are you blue with a crimson heart, or
are you crimson with a blue heart?

Agha Jan, I am 100 percent certain that theologians do not know
God. If they did there wouldn't be so many theology books. Did Jesus,
Moses and Mohammad (peace be upon them) go to theology school to
know God? Theologians don't know God is Alive. If they did they
would establish a direct communication with Him, like the Prophets

did. But I suppose they think they're above God; what is there that they don't know? After all, they profess to have studied God! Their god must definitely be limited, since apparently He knows not how to reveal himself to whomever He wants, and so people must go through them to know God. Agha Jan, one day You said, do You think that if Jesus came to Earth and wanted to go to the Vatican, he'd be granted an audience with the Pope? This statement certainly sparked our heads with clarity. So, I thought, if Jesus, Buddha, Moses or Mohammad (peace be upon them all) came and said, this is who We are, what would be our measure for recognizing them? Agha Jan, one day You said, what difference does it make if you say God, Allah, the Father, or Yahweh, what difference does it make if You don't know Him. Sit down and keep repeating bread, bread, bread, bread, does that stop your hunger? When people are hungry they don't care what name bread is called, they do something about it. How can you limit God to a name? And besides, how can you deny yourself of your fair share by just blindly repeating a name, behold the Face!

Agha Jan, I'll never forget the intellectual, arrogant woman, who thought she knew everything and could trick You into showing prejudice for Islam. How little she knew! As always, You put the matter so plainly and patiently to her that she became silent immediately. You told her, when You want to paint a painting what do you need? You need a canvas, you need brushes, paint, and of course the painter, and... Let's say this is the stage Moses was presenting to the human race. Next, you need to sketch the basic idea. Let's say, this is the stage Jesus was presenting to the human race. Next you need to put the colors in and give it a complete form. Let's say this is what the Prophet of Islam was presenting to the human race. Now tell me, which one is better than the other? To have the painting, you need all of them, and when the painting's complete, is there anything else to add? Look into your heart and ask God to reveal the Prophet of your time, so he can take you through all the stages for your painting to be complete! Agha Jan, thank You for Your patience.

You've said for people to obey the commandments of Jesus, they must first live the commandments of Moses. You said, Moses told people committing adultery is a sin, and Jesus said even thinking about adultery is a sin. Isn't it necessary to practice the commandments of Moses before you can abide by what Jesus said, and call yourself a Christian? You said, what people know of Islam is the distorted image painted to destroy it. People don't know that adultery in Islam is to be engaged in anything but the remembrance of God.

Agha Jan, I remember in a radio interview, You were asked about sin. You said, sin is anything that takes You away from balance—your true state. I thought a great deal about these words. I don't believe anyone has ever heard such a definition of sin. I recalled Your Beloved Father's words, "The true human being is the sky and earth that in balance lives." I realized that the key is balance. We must have the measure to have balance. Agha Jan, You are the measure and the balance. I know that; it's carved inside my heart, Agha Jan. How can we be in balance away from You?

Agha Jan, You also said, feeling guilty about anything is a sin. If you've done something that you shouldn't have done, learn from the experience, put it behind you and don't repeat it again. Does a smart person carry dead bodies on his shoulder? It's the ignorance of man-made religion that's brought about the concept of guilt. Don't forget the key is to be in the moment!

Agha Jan, You always tell people not to follow anyone, but to ask God to show them the Path. You always say these words from the Holy Book, "Don't follow that which you have no knowledge of." You always say, if God is absolute, then He is able to reveal to you the way to Him, so You will have certainty. Sit with a sincere and yearning heart, and ask God to show you the way to Him. You've tried all else, so what have you got to lose if you do as I say? Leave behind all beliefs you have, and let God reveal to you what you need to know.

Agha Jan, may those waves of ecstasy You send my way increase and increase ever more. Nonetheless, I know I must stay sober, for how could I ever get all my assignments done? Even when I sleep, I stay alert, afraid that the day may catch me unprepared. Agha Jan, I think I know why You give us assignments. If we're not engaged in remembering the Face of God, how else can we keep away from the alluring tricks of dust? You always give different assignments to each one of us. You are able to do everything Yourself. With the slightest flick of Your brow, everything will be as You wish it to be. So, it remains for us to solve, to be creative. How much of ourselves do we put into it—that's the test of creativity. No one ever knows what the others do. Agha Jan, is this because we each have to find ways to be creative? Is creativity stunned by knowing what others do? Agha Jan, You said, each person is unique, and must be cultivated for that uniqueness to be manifested. I suppose I have to present my fruit. Agha Jan, You once said, an apple tree can bear apples but not pears. But the apple tree can be cultivated and looked after so it can present the best apples, and the same holds true for the tree that bears pears. Agha Jan, isn't the fruit that we must bear oneness with You? Then how can each and every person be unique? Is the method of cognition unique to each person's experience? But I think the answer is this: You are total love, Agha Jan. Each fruit bears testimony to the love it has. So, it must be that You cultivate love within us, and that's the only way we can attain oneness with You.

Agha Jan, You said, read the Koran in Arabic, close it and wait, its meaning will be revealed to you. It is God's Book and He has the power to reveal it to You. This is why God's words do not need interpretation. When someone asked You about what he should do when he misses his prayer time, You said, do you rush to call the one you love, or wait till everything's done? If you've missed many meals, do you make up for it by eating all you've missed, or you eat what you need when the time's come. Agha Jan, I don't think he knew this Holy Verse, "Men whom neither traffic nor merchandise can divert from the remembrance of God, nor from regular Prayer." Agha Jan, You said, if you're praying and thinking of your mortgage, is the check for payment in front of you? The point is, do what is at hand, and do it with all your heart. Someone asked You, why is it necessary to pray five times a day? You said, don't you have to take antibiotics at their prescribed time for them to be effective?

Agha Jan, I always wish that I could see things the way You do. It must be so beautiful to see everything as it is. Agha Jan, You are so wonderful, beautiful. Everything You are. Agha Jan, the magnificence of Your presence, Your every gesture is perfection, grace, gentleness, kindness—the exquisite beauty of elegance and simplicity founded upon Knowledge, and so much more. Agha Jan, how can anyone ever attain the state of worshipping You? How can the drop of water ever know the greatness of the ocean, unless it immerses in it?

Agha Jan, I was thinking, You knew the Earth was round before anyone else, You knew everything before anyone discovered it. When people think they know a lot, they think they're God! After all, they don't stop and think that they did not create, but simply discovered what already existed. Did humans create the moon, the stars, energy, gravity, and so on? We're always reminded of who discovered what, but what about acknowledging the Evidence behind what's made scientists great? I guess the human ego ultimately takes its toll. Agha Jan, is there any way that You wouldn't have to bear the pain of witnessing human ignorance?

Agha Jan, it bothers me greatly when people use the word Sufi so loosely. They don't know that there can be but one Sufi in each age. Once I mentioned to You that when I mention Sufism, many people associate it with the dance. You said, people measure things by their own standards. The grocery store owner measures things by their weight, the mathematician through equations, and the philosopher by the weight of his words. So, those who are interested in the social aspects of what conventional religion offers are interested in the dance, others in the song. Who is truly searching for God? They don't know that the Sufi is the one who is totally annihilated and subsists in God. His every motion is that of God. The ecstasy flows from within and determines the movements from without, it's nothing that can be taught! Can you teach someone to love? Agha Jan, You've coined the definition of Sufism as the reality of religion. I haven't come across anyone who can understand it. But that's normal, isn't it? First, the definition of religion must be clarified, then the meaning of reality justified. Of course, all of this must be done in conjunction with clearing the mind of all of its imaginary conceptions of religion and God. Agha Jan, I haven't yet seen anyone who can define "*I.*" If they knew the reality of "*I,*" certainly they would know God.

Agha Jan, is it wrong to wish that when the time comes for me to shed my earthly shell I'd like to rest my head at Your Feet? You said, where will You go when this earthly shell finally drops. Do you know your proper home? Where will you go? Agha Jan, no one likes to think of death. You said, everyone is so busy being engaged in death, they have no time to expend for true life! You said, everyday things are clear examples. To gain any result, there's preparation involved. If you want to go on a trip, you try to make the safest, the most convenient and comfortable travel arrangements. You find out about the weather, the conditions, everything. What makes you think that preparations are not necessary for such a sure thing as death? It's a pity, You said, that the human being who is so curious takes his death so casually. Agha Jan, is it because humanity's been fed so much nonsense that everyone who thinks the slightest bit is just tired of anything that cannot be experimentally validated? Agha Jan, You always say that we don't have to go far to validate anything. We are the laboratory, the subject and the experimenter. Everything can be substantiated first hand right where we are. You said, just close your eyes. What do you see? That's how much you'll know of your life after death. The darkness of the grave is much the same way.

Agha Jan, You've imparted wisdom to me, and taught me about human nature, so that I may know the intentions behind people's actions. So much is involved that no one's aware of; people's understanding of human behavior is based only on action and reaction and nothing else. Just the other day, I was challenged by a psychotherapist about human identity. She said, human identity is based on what is projected from our external world. I said, if that's all there is to human identity, does that mean the newly born infant who cries when it's hungry, or has other needs to be met, has no identity? She paused and became silent. I could tell she knew she'd spent her years enrolled in the wrong school to learn about human identity. Agha Jan, I did tell her that everything I was telling her I had learned from You. I didn't want her to think that I had anything to do with the knowledge at my fingertips.

Agha Jan, I remember that another time You gave another example to a woman who was questioning the existence of God. You asked her if she had a sewing machine, a washer, a dryer, a stereo, etc.? She said, yes. Then You asked her if each came with directions for use. She said yes. Then You told her, if machines that are man-made need directions before they're properly used, don't you think you need to know how you've been made, so you can look after yourself with care? You asked, where is your direction for use? How many doctors and specialists do you need to go to before they can tell you what's wrong, that is, provided they know. Just think how many years they've studied and what expensive machinery they use to simply diagnose. Yet, you don't even know if they know your cure. Don't forget, it's the heart that first forms, then the brain cells and all the rest. So where is the best place to look if you want to know yourself and how you were made? The knowledge is right there! You said, the watchmaker made a watch. The watch was made to take count of time. Is the watch the watchmaker, or the manifestation of the watchmaker's knowledge? You added, don't forget the real purpose of the watch. It makes no difference if you've got diamonds and gold surrounding the watch. If the watch doesn't tell time, it's not a watch!

You paused when I asked You about an explanation on what people call "previous lives." You said, reflect, and you'll know the emptiness in the words they say. I thought and thought, and finally came up with the answer. Thank You, Agha Jan, for the answer. Receiving answers like this is called inspiration, is it not, Agha Jan? The oldest sibling had told me if you're truly sincere about discovering anything, keep reflecting, Agha Jan's bound to reveal its answer to You.

Agha Jan, scholars have coined those philosophers in the past whose brains have received enlightenment as "illuminists." If they only knew the truth behind it! Scientists and scholars still remain amiss of the connection between the brain and the universal waves. The harmony that must exist between the Universal Mind and the receiver for any discovery to be made is completely missed by them. Science would take leaps in every field if scientists would learn from You how to harness and use existing energies and fields of forces in any discovery—medicine, space, etc.

To be inspired by God, one must be in harmony with God. That's what You always say, Agha Jan. I remember You gave the example of the tuning fork. The first time I heard it I couldn't understand what You meant, until I went out and bought one. Then I realized what You meant by harmony is inherent in submission. Submission is a word that displeases people, they have so much trouble with this word, I said. Pity that people never stop and evaluate objectively, instead of being reactive to things. But I suppose one must have a constant point of reference to evaluate objectively, and how many have access to such clarity? People think submission equals suppression. Can anyone be limited by being in harmony with God? After all, Islam means submission to God, not to any other but God. Agha Jan, people must have a different definition of God. In explaining submission You said, suppose people with different backgrounds get on a jet plane, and want to go to a set destination. They put their trust in the pilot, for they don't know how to get there. Now are they followers? Or, they've simply realized that in order to get to their destination, they need the pilot as their guide? After all, this is what the pilot's been trained for!

Agha Jan, reincarnation as originally meant must be the moment-to-moment deaths while undergoing the spiritual states, and not what people have come to believe as returning to the world again and again until they're cleansed. I recall reading in Your Beloved Father's books, that when the seeker has found the Way, his steps are in constant births and deaths. People who believe in reincarnation must think that the fetus is lifeless, so by housing a homeless spirit it will have life. Besides, they don't even consider what that fetus will do with an overgrown spirit which failed to do what it needed to do while still on the earth. What use will the spirit of a thief be to an apple tree, or an ant to an elephant? Perhaps recycling is necessary to keep other planes safe! Besides, are these spirits waiting somewhere so a fetus can be placed in a certain place for them to enter it. Does this type of thinking mean that fetuses must be created for purification of wandering souls? Can creation be so helpless? I suppose these wandering spirits waiting for the fetus to be born must not be pro choice! People don't know that whatever they need, they have in this lifetime. What makes them believe that in coming back they're going to use them differently again? If these spirits are so smart, couldn't they have been smart enough to do what they needed before parting from the earth? And if it is God or Existence as they say, who guides them to come back, why can't He grant their release? Besides, we don't see anything ever repeated in Existence. Existence has no time to repeat, nor to stagnate, nor to wait— are we apart and separate from Existence?

Agha Jan, I remember You once said, whatever you're in remembrance of, that's what you worship, and that's your god. I see stickers on cars saying, I love my dog, I love my car, I love hamburgers, and so on....

Agha Jan, why do people insist on displaying their ignorance? No one who's ignorant of physics tries to explain the laws and theories and disprove the great scientists. Why do people take so much liberty with the words of God and His Prophets? They're always arguing about which one's better, which one's borrowed from the other and so on. Don't they know that to be a Prophet one must have a prerequisite, and that is submission to the will of God? If people are submitted, do they have anything of their own to say, or are they just a vehicle for the message of God? How can they possibly be wrong if they are the Messengers of God? It hurts me so to see people think they're doing a favor by listening to the message of God. Don't they know that God doesn't need humans? If God is needy, then the definition of God must be changed.

Agha Jan, as soon as these words of Your Beloved Father came to me, "The wise is he who attracts benefit and repels loss," You told us, ask the Generous for great things, He will give. It's Your loss if You ask for small things. What is the greatest thing to ask God? Obviously the answer is God. What can you possibly not have if you have God? Doesn't 100 include one through 99 as well? You asked, if you would be faced with God, what is it that you would ask of God? Agha Jan, no one even conjectures that such a thing is feasible, let alone have a question ready for God. Agha Jan, You've shown me that it requires a great deal of preparation for people to truly believe that God is not far.

Agha Jan, You know I've always asked God for God only. But after that statement You made how could I ask You for trivial things. One day I gathered enough courage to ask You for a remedy for a sudden eruption of acne that our sophisticated medicine wasn't able to remedy. Well, that night when I went to sleep I felt as if bees were nesting on my skin. When I looked in the mirror the next morning not a trace of it was to be seen. Thank You, Agha Jan. I also remember asking You for another silly thing. But that was when I wasn't even a toddler yet. I said I can't get the right price for my.... You said put an ad in. The next day people were lined up, each outbidding the other for the.... I know these are silly things, but You've been so patient with me. I remember the time I came to ask You permission to have my gall bladder taken out, because the doctor had said there were just too many stones. You looked me straight in the eyes for a while. Then You said, go for another check-up. I did. The results, to my doctor's complete surprise, were negative. Not a trace of the stones. I also remember that there was a period that I was so neglectful of my eating habits that signs of a bleeding ulcer had appeared. I had not told You a word about it.

I remember sitting before You. You placed Your finger on Your stomach and started pressing it. I became so sad, because I thought You weren't well. I prayed all night for Your health. Well, You were gone the next day, and my ulcer was healed. Agha Jan, the last time You pressed Your finger on Your upper chest, I immediately realized that I must have had something that I was unaware of. Thank You, Agha Jan. Just recently, I cut my left thumb to the bone, blood gushed out and my entire body pulsated with pain. I called Your name, the blood stopped pouring and the pain was gone. I went to the emergency room, the doctor was surprised that the cut was healing so fast. The only thing that remains is a bit of numbness on the right side of my thumb. I told this to a friend. A few weeks later she told me that her palm erupted with blisters from a burn. She said to herself that she would try what I'd done. So she called You from her heart. She said the blisters were gone. She asked me, you say you always call Agha Jan when in need, so what is God's role in this? What could I tell her, Agha Jan, she hasn't even reached the toddler age yet. So, I said, do you know God? She said, no. I said, then ask from the one who comes to your aid, until God's Face is revealed in your heart.

Agha Jan, I've asked You for healing for my friends, family and others whom I had not known. You've healed and helped them all. Whatever it has been, You've been always the Generous Bountiful Father. How can I ever get all these good doctors not to look at healing with a raised brow? Can't they realize that miracles can be explained scientifically? After all, is it pride or people's lives at stake? I remember having asked You to help a co-worker who was suffering from terminal cancer, or another whose wife had cancer of the uterus, or my friend's father for whom no hope remained, and there are so many others. They all got well. They were thankful when the healing took place. But why did they forget how they got well? I remember You said, there are few people who ask God for God. Others forget about God when their needs are fulfilled. But those who ask God for God, no matter what happens to them, they're still the lovers of God. These are the tests of God.

Agha Jan, the incidence with the AIDS patient has really taken its toll on me. But, I know through it You've taught me lessons that will be in my ears for all the years to be. Day and night I prayed, asking You for help. I said, he is young and made a mistake to turn his back to You, please help him now that the world's turned its face from him. You said, I gave him health when he was desolate and in pain from his childhood days. Parents, women and others had abused him. I gave him strength and self-confidence, and then he said, now I'm ready to go into the world and discover what the world has in store for me. How do you know that once he gets well he won't turn his back again? He says that I am his hope and all he wants to do is to be at my call. The doctors have said there's no hope left, he saw his mate die in agony from AIDS. Now he's afraid of the pain here, and the uncertainty of the hereafter. At least now that he's saying he wants to come back, I'll take him through the darkness of the hereafter when his life ends here. But if I heal him now and he turns his back, he'll never see me again. My prayer changed after Your words. I said, God, give him what is best for him, his agony's great, I can hear the echo of death in his voice; I'm not asking for healing, but make his pain less, give him what is best, for Thou art the Merciful, the Compassionate, the Tender, the Gentle. Agha Jan, I had totally surrendered, but was suffocating from his pain—I could hear his life moving to the very edge. Just then You sent Your directions. Thank You, Agha Jan. How many times have I seen that You bring to life the dead! Where are his parents, who begged me to pray and ask You for help? They've taken their donations and their thanks to their church, where they said their "God" blessed them. You always say, it matters not if they know how the healing took place, what matters is for the patient to get well. I keep telling myself when will you realize that God guides whomever He wants, however He wants, whenever He wants!

Agha Jan, the utmost joy is to call You from the innermost chamber of my heart. I asked You for You, and asked that You take away whatever separates me from You. Now I know whatever comes my way has Your blessings, and whatever doesn't, is still Your blessings, Agha Jan.

Agha Jan, in this day and age everyone consults consultants for just about everything. Why are they surprised when I tell them I must ask You for everything and about everything? They don't realize how many times during one single day they ask people for advice. Men are the advisors of men. The entire society works on an advisory capacity. Can't they see the state of the world? Why can't people admit that there must be a Universal Mind capable of proper design. They don't need to look far, the human system attests to that, let alone nature and the universe. But I guess everyone still is stuck in the stone age mentality. Agha Jan, if only they knew what I know. Thank You, Agha Jan.

Agha Jan, the first time I heard this saying from the Lord of believers, I was totally heartbroken. He said, there was no one who truly listened to what He said, so He would go and talk into a well. I suppose the well reflects back in echo what one says, while earth-bound humans are like stone walls, no depth for the words to resound. I remember You once said, Jesus said, they have eyes but they do not see, they have ears, but they do not hear. You said, Jesus was a Prophet, He knew people have eyes and ears and some kind of action-reaction takes place. You said, what Jesus was referring to was a different hearing and a different seeing. Agha Jan, do You also go and talk into deep dark wells?

Agha Jan, do You think that the theologians and "holy people" think that Buddha, Moses, Jesus, and Mohammad (peace be upon them all) met the prerequisites to be Prophets?

Agha Jan, I have a feeling that if people were asked who knew more, the Prophets or Einstein, they'd say Einstein. This is how God and His Prophets are conceived in human minds! How well God and His Prophets are represented by those who profess to be Their representatives! Humans bring suit against misrepresentation.

Agha Jan, Your love grows more and more in my heart. Is that possible? I remember one of the exquisite lines in Your Holy Book that we chanted in Your Presence. I begged to be given one drop of that love, so that I would get a taste of that state You speak of. O' Agha Jan, please bless me with all Your Love. I yearn to be fully absorbed in Your Love, Agha Jan. Agha Jan, love is the remedy for everything. Even on the earthly plane, when we're in love everything looks different, everything seems easier, we become more tolerant and patient. What has changed? The lens is the same, but it's our state that's changed. Agha Jan, wouldn't human suffering that's caused by people's hurting and hoarding be diminished if hearts would be filled with the love of God? Agha Jan, wouldn't our standards for need change if there weren't the need to prove anything or compete with anyone? If we find inner peace and contentment, and if we have inner strength, how would we view the world, what would our relationships be like? Agha Jan, You said our love for God should shine through our actions.

Agha Jan, I remember once You said, if I say something, and there's even a trace of disagreement in you, it means that you're not submitted. How I've tried to cover up my objections. You always say to Your children that we don't love You. Naturally, we all immediately object. We think we love You. Agha Jan, will we ever know how much You care and love us? Why are we blind and deaf? Who said ignorance is bliss! Submission of the limited "self" is what brings bliss. Agha Jan, will You bless me with this gift?

Agha Jan, people ask me to pray for them, for their problems or ill health to go away. Whenever I pray, I ask Your permission first, I say, "In God's Great Name" and that's when You take over, and they get well, or have their needs met. Thank You, Agha Jan.

Agha Jan, once You said, look at airplanes, when they want to take off they have to get clearance and the same holds true when they want to land. All the time they're in the sky, they still have to keep watch and keep in touch. You said, that's why the Holy Prayer is said. You are asking God for permission to take off. He has to give You permission and guide each step of the way, so your journey can be safe and your destination to Him be made.

Agha Jan, just the other day one of the siblings said that the siblings are jealous of me. Do You remember how one of them tried to poke my eyes out the night You gave Your speech on *Peace*, had You not intervened? Well, everyone wants all of Your love and attention and doesn't want it to be shared. They don't know that the more they share, the more You give. Will the ocean run dry if a few of its drops fill a cup? How many cups can the ocean fill up, and still be the ocean and fill more cups?

Agha Jan, the first year I entered Your Holy School, You said, if you become the most learned person in the world, at best you'll be remembered in books which are placed on library shelves. If you become the most wealthy, when death calls you at last, will gold and silver redeem your life? If you become the most powerful, at best they'll call streets and cities after your name. Decide what it is that you want. The answer seemed clear enough to me, but I wondered why Agha Jan had said all this. I knew that a pact was to be made, and if I broke the pact I would never set my eyes on Agha Jan again. My decision was made.

Agha Jan, to this day, it's been You who's pulled me through, to keep the pact in place. Please don't leave me to myself, Agha Jan. If only I could remember this in times when I'm put through the tests.

Agha Jan, one day one of Your older children told me, value yourself. You're Agha Jan's treasure chest. At first, deadly pride showed its face. But I quickly brushed it away and focused on the meaning behind what he said. I knew his comment wasn't in vain. I realized that You've given me so many jewels: ruby, and that's affection; emerald, and that's compassion; pearls, and that's brotherhood; sapphire, and that's abundance; turquoise, and that's serenity; and diamond, which is colorless, and that is love. Your teachings are priceless, but I think what he really meant is that my heart is in my chest. Where is the abode of God but in one's heart, Agha Jan?

Agha Jan, You know the well known poet-woman who is charming and joyful, the one I truly like, and whose mischievous ways are just a delight. She always introduces me to everyone as the Sufi princess. The first time she said that I was truly shocked. I tried to find ways to nicely tell her that I should never be praised. Then one day, as I began to tell her, You sent my heart a message. I realized she had tuned in to what had not crossed my mind. Of course I am a Sufi princess. Am I not Your child? You are the King, the absolute total King, the one and only King. So how can Your children bear not Your heritage?

Agha Jan, I was thinking the other night about the beautifully prayer-calligraphied cloths that we spread on the floor at meals, and I suddenly realized why that was done. It's to remind us that our daily bread for the body and soul comes only from You. Humans need reminders all the time, since we're forgetful. How could we have forgotten that we belong in heaven, and our home's not the earth? I recall the beautiful poem by Your Beloved Grandfather:

> *Bird of Paradise I am*
> *To this earth I belong not*
> *This body's been made a cage*
> *Just for a brief few days.*

And of course I chant daily Your exquisite poem:

> *Unfold my wings, set me to fly,*
> *From the fortress of these dungeon walls,*
> *My liberation grant.*

Agha Jan, one day when I was walking by Your side in the garden holding little Nirvana in my arms, You said, you have to be so well prepared that you'll never have to worry about preparing for class again. Right after that, I quickly started making preparations. But as soon as I went to the first class I realized that as I begin it is You who takes over. You said "be" and so it is to this day, 11 years later.

Agha Jan, one day I came to You and said, people keep insisting that the Holy Book discriminates against women. You said, ask them, is the soul female or male? God's words are meant for the soul and not for the body which is classified by gender. It's the ignorant who make such applications. You said, have you seen an illiterate person pick up any book and explain its contents? Only fools allow themselves such pastures!

Agha Jan, in my diary I wrote one night, when I was truly forlorn, I wished I could be a bird and sit by Your window and just watch You all the time. But then I realized, how could my frail wings keep up with Your travels far and wide? Then, I thought there must be a better way. So I said, what could I be so I would never be separated from You? I finally decided that if only I could find a way into Your heart and just settle there, I'd always be protected from separation. Agha Jan, is that possible? Agha Jan, will You always keep me in Your heart?

Agha Jan, You always say closeness is not in physical proximity, but in inner connectedness. Agha Jan, why is it that Your oldest children, those who've past through the most difficult stations and states, and left behind all their earthly belongings and entered Your heavenly kingdom, long for You even more? The pain of separation I can hear in their voice, their voice brings tears out of a stone. Agha Jan, is longing and yearning because of our captivity in the earthly mold? But I've read in the Holy Book, that unless annihilation in God takes place here, we must bear the pain of separation through our journey henceforth. Agha Jan, will I ever be completely absorbed in You? How can a thorn be absorbed in pure mist? Only mist can be absorbed in mist. So I must totally burn in the fire of Your love, Agha Jan.

Agha Jan, why are midnight-blue Irises in wheat fields at dusk so exquisitely beautiful? It must be because they remind me of You, Agha Jan.

Agha Jan, is the heart's core like a crystal? It must be. From all angles I see Your Face reflected on it. Do crystals reflect the echoes of love? It must be, since everything I see or hear resounds Your Presence.

Agha Jan once You said, "I am alone." Everyone became sad, we thought this means no one is favored by You. I've given it some thought and realized that of course You're alone. Not to be alone means that one must have another equal to oneself in every respect. How can there ever be two Agha Jans? Another time, when a few of us were gathered around You for breakfast, You said, no one can ever please me. Well, Your ever tender heart couldn't see our hearts shrivel up like burnt marshmallows at what You'd said. So, You added, for anyone to please Me, they'd have to be just like Me. But of course, there can never ever be two Agha Jans!

Agha Jan, does the essence of the Mohammadi Rose revive the one who has fainted, because it brings the fragrance of the Beloved to the heart?

Agha Jan, You once said, among all of you I am the least experienced. But of course You are, how can Absolute Knowledge need experience to know anything? Experience is for earthly creatures who learn through trial and error and try to establish acceptable means for exchange.

Agha Jan, when I first came to Your Holy School I was afraid of Your Beloved Grandfather, of whom it is said, "If it hadn't been for our Lord Mohammad ibn Abolfazl Angha, the reality of Sufism would never have been revealed in our era." His photograph seemed so stern that I always avoided His Eyes. One night during meditation, He appeared and so kindled His love in my heart that during prayers I can always see His loving Eyes, and it's so easy to put my head at His Feet when I'm tired. Does He favor the fragrance of gentle pink carnations? So often at different times of day or night, suddenly I can touch the most sublime scent of carnations in the space around me, and I know He's present. I wonder why lilies of the valley also remind me of Him?

Agha Jan, each flower must reveal the fragrance of God. Are there more than 124,000 fragrant flowers? Your Fragrance is so dear to my heart. I've always loved Persian violets. I remember as a child I'd go to a stream where there were fields of violets, I'd walk in between all the flowers making sure I wouldn't hurt them. I had a spot where I could easily lie down and inhale their exquisite fragrance without disturbing them. I always prayed that God would protect them from all the passersby. And of course, I immediately recognized that "languishing fragrance" as soon as I entered Your House, Agha Jan.

Agha Jan, not once, but many times You've said, close your eyes, so you can see God inside your hearts. How can anything that goes on outside be more important than beholding God in your heart? Agha Jan, Agha Jan, if only they knew what I know, how could they ever take their eyes away from You?

Agha Jan, most people who want to start Your Path ask, do I have to leave everything behind? What do I have to give up? You've always said, what do you do when children don't want to part with what's bad for them? If you take it away abruptly they scream and cry, if you take it away gently, they want it back, but if you give them something better in exchange, they let go of it rather fast. I wish I could tell them, why don't you grow up. What is more valuable than meeting God? I should ask them, does a smart person hang on to glass when given a diamond in hand? Well, most people don't understand this. But I don't care. My duty's merely to announce, for the guidance comes from God.

Agha Jan, once I confronted a woman who wanted to debate about God. I said, before you continue, stop and ask yourself, what purpose would it serve you to know God? She left without saying a word further. She came back a few days later, and to this day she remains as one of Your children. Agha Jan, there's no telling how You guide whomever You want!

So many nations fight one another saying it's to protect God's name and command. Is God so helpless that He needs humans to protect His name? Or, is He so needy that He needs others to interpret His words? I guess they're too afraid to say they use Your name to fill their pockets with gold and rule people through promises and fears. After all, if anything goes wrong, it's Your Name at stake, and not theirs. Agha Jan, I know You don't care. There You stand, Majestic and Grand. You brush these things away as flies. The newest religion is the invention of politics. It's coined as a universal religion, one of brotherhood, of peace and so forth, everything that's appealing to people is in it. And of course, it focuses on social exchanges so they can gather people together. After all, people like to have a good time. But where's the seal of God on it? I've read all their documents, all the handwritten letters, and all the rest. I guess religion and politics go hand in hand, the best way to manipulate ignorant minds. Agha Jan, is that why You insist that we learn and learn, and pass on the teachings to whomever wants to learn? Agha Jan, I recall Your Beloved Father's words, "The least you'll learn by coming to this School, is never to be fooled by anyone again."

Agha Jan, politics seem like children at play. One day they're friends, the next they're enemies. They can never decide who's on whose side. Agha Jan, I remember once You said, human nature doesn't change if it's not trained. Then it must be that people like to play games, but their tools get bigger and deadlier so they can live their whims. It's the naive and the greedy who engage in the game. Agha Jan, You said, the way world leaders rule is to keep people busy at certain games, while they themselves are busy planning the next exploitation game.

Agha Jan, in our classes and at meals, we always sit on the floor, never at a table. Outsiders always object to this. They say, our backs hurt, our legs go numb. When I asked You what to say to them, You said, tell them, do soldiers get trained by being pampered? For sure, You train us as soldiers, to guard against the unruly "self." But how many want to be soldiers? The smart ones know that this body's term's bound to be up, so they seek to know the "I" that the body inhabits. The smart ones don't give up the search for the lasting "I," while the neglectful ones tend more and more to what's obvious and is not going to last.

Agha Jan, I was thinking that if psychologists and psychiatrists would read all this, they'd think I was a true case of multiple personalities. Little do they know that they too would go through all this to get to the true personality.

Agha Jan, to each of Your children You give a coin with special prayers engraved on it. It's meant to keep us safe from harm and pain. But I've also discovered why we wear them around our necks. Silver turns black through contact with air. It has to be polished to keep its shine. This is a reminder for us to keep all else out of our hearts, so Your love shines through our hearts.

Agha Jan, just a few more hours before we arrive. So many children are flocking to see You from all over the world. Agha Jan, why are planes ever so slow? I know nothing equals love's wings in speed.

Agha Jan, do pride, jealousy, envy and arrogance clip one's wings of flight, and stop the learning process that provide the fuel for flight? The Path is one of love, the journey's love, and what is learned is true love. Is this correct, Agha Jan? If it's pride, envy, arrogance and jealousy that people want, they've come to the wrong door, no such nourishment's to be found at Agha Jan's door. For sure, Agha Jan strips you of all your earthly scars, so that love may heal them all. Agha Jan, so many times I nearly drowned in pain, but before my last breath, You gently pulled me through it again with tender loving care. Just the slightest hint that You care sends us into orbit, where no human eye is allowed to set its gaze. I wish one day You would reveal all the mysteries to me... but I suppose they're far ahead. Agha Jan, You've said the last stage on this journey is where all mysteries are revealed to the sincere. But Agha Jan, what mystery is left to know when the veil has been lifted from the Face of God? What more can I aspire to, when Your Face shines within my heart, Agha Jan.

Agha Jan, on the physical plane, adolescence is a time when the person wants to establish his or her own identity and authority and announce independence. Did You just put me through and pull me out of adolescence on the spiritual plane? I think I've noticed the same symptoms in some of the other siblings as well. Did adolescence begin when You made us think that we were the ones doing it all—making the decisions, knowing what to do—and the strength and power was ours? It did go to our heads. We thought we were somebodies! We forgot that we came to You, to lose our self-importance and not to pick up excess luggage. So another stage is past. Thank You, Agha Jan, for putting us through the experience, so we would find out with strength and faith that You are the Doer, and our every moment on You depends. What comfort, what freedom this is.

Agha Jan, You've said, I'm closer to you than your jugular vein. This entire body functions as a heart and each cell pulsates from the pulse of the heart, so where is it that You are not, Agha Jan?

Agha Jan, night has arrived, and Your children are asleep. Their faces are peaceful, content and love-filled by You. I heard Your footsteps and saw the sparkle of Your love settle over them and surround them in a halo of light. You gave each a special gift. As for me, You put me to sleep before giving my special gift. Agha Jan, it's dawn now, and another hour before we're at Your side.

Agha Jan, our homes are now so dark, after being engulfed in Your light. It's dismal and lonely unless You fill the emptiness with Your light.

Agha Jan, there must have been at least 1,200 of us at Your side. We had put on our best white clothes. We came prepared to absorb and absorb from all over the world. We had lined up from sunrise to get the best seats, so we could get the best view of You. My wish was granted, I was given the best possible seat. I had full view of Your eyes, as well as being so close by. The room was filled to the brim, others had to be seated in the adjoining rooms with closed circuit T.V. Although I felt sad, because they were separated from us and couldn't be in Your presence, I later learned that they had close up views of You. Agha Jan, You always bless everyone equally, no matter where they are. Some who were watching You through the closed circuit T.V. said they peeked during the chants, although that's the time everyone's forbidden to open their eyes. You always say, look within. But, Agha Jan, can

You blame them for taking advantage of this chance unique? To look at You from full view for six full hours isn't a chance to be missed. Well, You know I was moved from my prime place and was placed in the corner facing the wall. So, I kept my eyes closed all the while, well, my heart had sunk by that time.

I wanted to look at this masterpiece so elegant and simple. I had wanted to see it, since I had heard that it was designed and its construction supervised by You. Simplicity and elegance based upon knowledge is perfection. Is that correct Agha Jan? So how can anything done at Your Hands be anything but perfect? Nature certainly bears testimony to that! No sound system was needed, the tiniest sound could be heard. Agha Jan, I wish I could have gotten a lengthier look. I felt right at home, as if I'd been there many times before. I wished and wished that I could be there always at Your side.

Time for Your arrival arrived. My ears were glued to the door all the while, at least I would get a quick glimpse if I could detect when You'd arrive. I know Your footsteps even if they're miles away. Before they announced Your arrival, I was ready to jump up. Agha Jan, why are we so deprived of seeing You? When one of the siblings came back and went to work she was asked by a co-worker if she was suffering from jet-lag, because she looked so dazed. Of course, she responded, the jet lag from heaven to earth is indeed great!

Agha Jan, You didn't even give us a chance to indulge for a second to absorb Your Presence. The twinkle in our eyes vanished, and our eyelids drooped as You quickly began Your training—scolding us so severely. We became desolate, we said, we've failed Agha Jan again. You said, when are you going to learn not to take candy from strangers? Don't you know that these people wear the Sufi garb to trick you? Agha Jan, Your voice was tired and disappointed. You made no exceptions, no one was spared. I remember, You once said, if you want a donkey to move, you have to make sure he sees the spears. Is that why You were scolding us, Agha Jan? I guess our earthly mold had really thickened, how else do You train donkeys who are drawn to water and straw?

Nothing can ever make us behave but the fear of disappointing You, Agha Jan.

Agha Jan, You gave us much to think about. You spoke of the seven days of creation, and how to find our place in these seven days. You spoke to us of the necessity of the Messenger and the Holy Teacher and their role in preparing humans to reach the seventh day of creation for the divine birth to take place.

You spoke of becoming purified of our earthly traits, to become ready for the seventh day of creation. That's when godly traits are manifest—Knowledge, Wisdom, Compassion, Love, and so much more. We certainly realized that we were at the very base of that ladder, nowhere near the divine traits. Agha Jan, who else but God, His Messenger, and His designated Teacher can be there? You said, when the first sign of growth takes place, that's God's will, but God must introduce the Messenger to purify and cleanse you of Your earthly appetites, and then the Holy Teacher imbues You with His breath so your creation can be completed, so you return to your Origin. Amen, Agha Jan.

Agha Jan, for the first time You told us about the secret behind our circles of *Zekr* (chants of remembrance). If only I could have a recording of Your Voice saying the *Zekr*, then that red-hot charcoal will certainly keep my heart sparked with love. Agha Jan, Your Voice always reminds me of the verse in the *Psalm of the Gods*, "...whispering the Psalm of the Gods calmly, in perfect tenderness, soothing to the eager ears of the Sons of Man."

Agha Jan, You said, what difference is there between a newspaper and the Holy Book, if your faith is based on words? Seek the reality behind the words. What is the measure for knowing the truth but truth? Are the tools used by the dentist viewed equally useful by the plumber as the dentist? Each sees, evaluates and uses the tools according to his own knowledge. So what is the measure that is constant and can be called the Truth?

You told us how we shouldn't be content with just growing roots.

You said this body is like roots, stop indulging in it, fruit grows not on roots. Certainly roots serve goats quite well. For the growth process to be complete, roots, branches, leaves and fruit all are necessary. One without the other is incomplete. Agha Jan, You said, if you ask people why they eat they say, not to be hungry. The reason you eat is to get the proper nourishment for growth, not merely to grow roots.

Agha Jan, You said, one day a man came and said, I've carried everyone's loads and tended to them, now God should pay my recompense. You told him, you've served others, now you ask God for your pay? You said it's like the story of a man who was paid to deliver watermelons to a certain place, when returning he kept grumbling that they should have given him the skins at least. Agha Jan, people can never get things straight in their heads. They can't be blamed, so much superstition and ignorance fills their heads when it comes to religion and God. Well, this person's attitude reminded me of people who boast that they've given their lives to the human cause, they've served the needy and the poor, etc. They're regarded by others as men of God. I don't understand how God ever entered the picture here. It's not uncommon to hear that he's so pious, he's given his life in the work of God, he's helped the orphans, the homeless and the sick! Helping others is a must—that's what You teach us—but what does that have to do with the worship of God? I remember reading in Your Beloved Father's Holy Book, "If people are honest, adhere to all the social laws and agreements, do not base their beliefs on blind obedience, and yet do not have a religion, will they lose?"

Agha Jan, You asked, when will you learn not to confuse things? Going hungry, not sleeping, all the supposedly ascetic things that are to bring closeness to God, are not what people think they are. Closeness to God has no physical links. Of course, you must have control over your natural appetites so you can collect, focus and direct your energies and powers for the worship of God. I said to myself, closeness to God has no physical links, but how I love to sit and sit and watch and watch

You, mesmerized, Agha Jan! You caught my thought and paused. Then You said, but when someone's totally absorbed in beholding the Face of God, does he try to stay away from food, or does he take a break to go and eat? There's a big difference between trying to fall in love and being in love!

Agha Jan, You gave an example that my brain cells just burned. You said, does a seed look for a gardener to plant it and tend to it. If it knew so much then it wouldn't need a gardener. People go in the streets looking for a Teacher. Your Teacher, Your Prophet must be introduced by God if he's to lead you to God. You said, does a baby in a womb search for and choose a doctor, or ask to have parents?

You said the essential thing is for you to separate yourself from your earthly shell. The journey of the true self is different than the colony of cells. The dead skin is peeled off when you cleanse yourself. The dead cell's life journey is now different from the living cells. Your body is a piece of machinery for travel on Earth. People don't travel on sea with the automobile. To travel on sea you need the ship; to travel the skies you need the airplane. Develop the means of travel before the body's time is up! The animal traits too must be peeled off for the soul to journey towards God. Now tell me, how can you have a teacher who's not God-sent? Agha Jan, You said, take a cut flower, it appears that it is alive. But is it really? It was cut from its source of life, and in a few days it'll show that it has no life. Agha Jan, You said, when an unripe apple falls to the ground, can you connect it back to the branch? Agha Jan, does this mean that humans run around while dead?

You said, you're here for a few hours, then you'll go back. Which one of you burned your home and did away with all you had? You left everything in its place, and you do have a place for return. Why don't you think that there's a place of return after you've shed your shells? Where is that home that you must find? It's only a gambler who puts his house and everything else at stake!

Agha Jan, You asked, do you know why you're here, and what you must do? Is there any time left to get entangled in disputes? Take heed, hold sacred what you're about, know yourself, for God's work is never done in jest.

Agha Jan, You said, people so easily get trapped in the rituals they're offered in the place of truth. They're happy to give their money and lives, and take away loads of ignorance with them. Your loads are taken away, and you're given spiritual gifts, but you come thinking I owe you something. The sleepless nights, the concerns have been mine, You said. Well, you deserve to go to those healers of the soul who gather in their opium dens, and the teacher drinks whisky and passes the opium around to those who've passed his tests. That's what you all deserve! You said, I'm like a bankrupt farmer who has spent all his time and energy planting, plowing and tending, but pests and drought reap the harvest of his toil.

You said, I'm just tired of the lot of you. Be gone, and don't come around. Well, Agha Jan, by unanimous vote we all agreed that unless You scold us this way, we'll never let go of our earthly shells. Agha Jan's tired of staying on Earth to watch over us. He wants us to fly. Wishful thinking, said one of the younger ones. What audacity, what nerve, the rest of us jumped at him. We don't want to hear any of your silly talk. After all, Agha Jan scolds us because He really cares and loves us all. Agha Jan, today as I was driving, a stone sharply hit the windshield. Immediately fright went right through me, and all my inner chatter stopped. I suddenly thought, under threat, all idleness immediately stops. Is that the reason You scolded us? To flush away all the excesses we brought, so we could be prepared to absorb all the blessings we were being bestowed?

Agha Jan, I remember You used to have a beautiful rosary. I always thought that each bead was one of Your children. What else ties us and connects us together, but Your love? Agha Jan, I haven't seen Your rosary lately, does that mean You're not praying for us anymore?

Agha Jan, at one point You paused; it was a long pause. It was right in the middle of Your explanation on Creation. You said, when I pause, be sure that some ill-thought is occupying a mind. Well, I could hear everyone quickly tighten up all their brain cells, and fold over their eyelids and sit real straight. The next time You paused, You said, I know how to drink tea. Don't forget there's no one who can train me, or teach me anything. Well, I immediately knew that there was a stray bird among us. Your children know all that, Agha Jan. There's nothing You don't know. How can anything be added to Absolute Knowledge? At Your third pause, my heart simply stopped. I said, You'll leave and never look back again, Agha Jan.

Agha Jan, I was quite happy when the older brother asked for penitence for all the rest, and in earnest asked that You never ever turn Your Face away. And another one said, don't judge us by our shortcomings, but look at Your generosity, Agha Jan. Of course, I've also learned the trick lately. The one who has the occasion to offer the prayers is in a position to present all the supplication his heart desires, for You're listening. He can say words of adoration, worship and so much more, there's no other occasion that one can be even a tiny bit bold. Who would dare say, Agha Jan, You're the essence of beauty and grace, that Your beauty simply captivates me, and enraptures me, and....?

Agha Jan, true love as You know, we don't know. But, we love and adore You the best way we know. No matter how hard You scold us, we still come back for more. Our skins have thickened from the scoldings You give us, but our hearts are warm and tender from the love You give us.

Agha Jan, all Your children were displaying their best to please You. Everyone wants to be the best behaved. On the way back, one of my siblings said, there was an overgrown child who kept sliding her foot underneath hers. Pretty soon my sibling could neither sit, nor kneel, she was in mid-air. Your anger was aroused and You said, how many times have I said that unless these children are well trained they're not to come to the gathering yet. Agha Jan, it was obvious that she hadn't even reached the toddler age. Even toddlers know they can't stretch out their legs; at best, it's the little toe they can stretch. Agha Jan, I've compared notes with all those who sit still and never budge. They say, the trick is to sit still and let the legs go numb from pain. The body's then forgotten, then one can concentrate. Agha Jan, my legs ached and ached, but never went numb.

Agha Jan, You said, to this date I've never abused anyone's right. I didn't understand what You meant. How can Absolute Knowledge abuse anyone's right? I remember in this context You said, people interpret the Holy Words based on their own mental frame. From justice they think everyone must have equal rights, enjoy good health, have equal numbers of hairs on their heads, not suffer from natural disasters, not fall down if drunk, not be subject to child abuse, rape, and so forth. You said, whenever something goes wrong, God is always blamed, and when things go right, of course it's the human will and mind that take the credit. You said, people don't know that justice is the word for scale, measure, balance. You said, this means there's something unique about each entity in the universe. Look at nature, does a tree say I want to be a creek? The reason is, nature's mysteries are revealed in each and every particle. That's how they're submitted, manifest their uniqueness, and exist in total harmony. For humans, the same holds true, but humans are so engaged in what goes on outside of them that they're not in touch with the measure that gives them the balance so they can manifest their uniqueness as well. Agha Jan, You said, discover your uniqueness so you will know the meaning of God's justice.

Agha Jan, You said, people say they're psychologists and they heal the human "psyche," and they draw parallels between their work and man's quest for God. You said, all they do is work with the nerves, nerves are like trees. How can they show the way to God by manipulating the behavior that results from the reactivity of nerves? Others say, they're spiritual healers, their work is to heal the human soul. If the soul is God's Breath, then how can it need healing? Since they can't even differentiate between the different aspects of the human being, how can they even aspire to heal and remedy it? Even assuming that the soul was to be healed, where is their certificate that shows God has sealed it? Aren't medical certificates sealed by authorities? You said, in the old days, the older women served as the local therapists, everyone came to them and troubles were aired-away, and each was comforted. No other claim was ever made.

You said, healing the "human-self" and cleansing it needs the hand of the Prophet of Time, who's introduced to each person in need, inwardly by God. If a person's hungry and asks his neighbor for bread, is he served stones instead? How can God be less than the neighbor to His children who ask in earnest to be helped? Ask God in earnest to show you the Way. One thirsty for water doesn't settle for the desert mirage. Can one's thirst be quenched by the mirage? Charlatans wearing the garb of truth always look for seekers like you, but if you're thirsty, you will not settle for anything but the Truth.

Agha Jan, then the Prophet of Time is God manifest on Earth, and the Holy Teacher His Breath, so all are One. Each name designates the level with which God's teachings are revealed to man. Is this correct, Agha Jan?

Agha Jan, I must make a confession. After the Holy Visit a few of us gathered and started to compare notes. One sibling said you should never stare at Agha Jan. I said, staring is rude, but how can you not gaze at Agha Jan? If I don't look at Agha Jan, I simply don't understand what goes on. To make sure I was not making a big mistake, I checked with the oldest sibling who has the longest white beard, who knows by heart every word in the 150 books that Your Beloved Father has written, as well as all those books written by You, and has written verses for every word in all the books. I guess he must be Your only true child. He said, what's wrong if the gaze is a loving gaze? Gaze all you want, while you can. How often is it that you have a chance to be in the presence of the Almighty One? My heart rested, for I hadn't taken my eyes away even for a split-second from Your Beauteous Countenance. That was the time when a few of us were allowed to remain behind, to receive Your very special instructions. Agha Jan, thank You for giving me sustenance for at least one winter day. My greed to be in Your Presence is never satisfied, it simply increases every day.

Agha Jan, I'm always amazed to see how many non-Persian speaking people sit for hours in Your Presence. One day I checked with one Swiss girl. She said afterwards she always discusses with her fiancé (who is Persian) what went on, and he is always amazed at how much sharper the images are that she receives. Agha Jan, is that the state You refer to in Your interview on *The Secret Word*, "the brain is disconnected?" The state where the boundary of language does not exist, because the speaker is God, and God's words reach the heart?

Agha Jan, sometimes You send Your envoys in disguise to test the strength of our faith and how well we hold the house-secrets intact. Sometimes we're strong and sometimes we're weak, but when it comes to guarding the One Secret from all ears, we put our lives at stake in Your Name, Agha Jan. Agha Jan, sometimes I think I could get lynched easily. No price is too much for the value of my head—the archive of secrets undivulged! Agha Jan, I fear no one. My Protector is You. My Guardian is You. I've asked none all these years for anything but You. You've given me whatever's been best for me. How many people can claim such confidence? To stand firm for what they say? Never fearing anything—ill health, grief, pain, nor death. Agha Jan, please don't take Your Hand away.

Agha Jan, now we're counting the days until February 4th, our other annual Pilgrimage. This time we'll really be prepared. Our hearts will really shine. Perhaps we needed more preparation, more midnight vigils to cleanse our hearts. We received our special midnight lamps on Your birthday, September 30th. It wasn't enough time until the 17th of November for our hearts to be wiped clean, but now since the work's been started, by February we'll really please You, Agha Jan.

Agha Jan, after You scolded us, we were glad. We thought, we don't want to live as beasts. You said God's words are these, "And when he became stable, I imbued him with My Spirit." We certainly don't want to settle for any less than that, when we can inherit Your qualities divine. Agha Jan, how many scoldings must we get before we can attain that state? Agha Jan, a newly grown tree, its bark is smooth, while a tree that's been tended to and learned to stand tall and firm, its skin is weathered and coarse. It's learned not to bend to the events of time. Is this a correct comparison, Agha Jan?

Agha Jan, You told us that when a tree is growing, it needs to be pruned. Who determines when, where and how? It's the gardener and not the tree. Do you want to grow, be firm and bear the best fruit? Agha Jan, my jasmine tree that I've been growing for You bears testimony to Your words.

Agha Jan, one of the siblings said that his oldest brother who would receive instructions from Your Beloved Father would say, "Whenever the Master smiled at us and was kind, I came home and cried, whenever he scolded us I came home and smiled." Well, the dear little one must have thought his brother was really confused. But the brother had explained that when the Master scolded it meant that He cared, he said he worried about the days Your Beloved Father smiled and did not say much.

Agha Jan, we had one last theory on why You scolded us, and that was to make the pain of parting much less. Thoughts of ways on how to please you drive laments of separation away, and certainly keep us out of mischief as well. Is this another wishful thought, Agha Jan?

Agha Jan, my bags are packed and I've bathed for days in the Thai sea and sun, ready for the Holy Pilgrimage—4th of February! What a surprise, Agha Jan. In the middle of the desert where no habitation was in sight, the most beautiful majestic white tent was placed to welcome the pilgrims from all over the world. A satellite system would take Your message to the four corners of the world—for those who couldn't come.

Just to think, we were only an hour from L.A. The local siblings were really showing off with the preparations they'd made to welcome the rest of us.

Tents have one advantage over walls. Shadows can be detected from without. I quickly spotted Your Majestic Stance and rose up before Your arrival was announced. As You know, I was suffering from jet lag as well as time lag. I tightened my muscles next to the other siblings so I wouldn't fall on my face. But, Agha Jan, Your words I recalled regardless of my physical condition.

You're always different on this Holy Day than the rest of the days. After all, it's Your Beloved Father's Birthday. But this time I could detect a shadow of sadness. Agha Jan, thank You for granting my wish, now we have been blessed with the video containing all that You imparted to us on that blessed Day. It's interesting that the video confirms that if You want someone to know something nothing stands in the way. The video confirms that I had registered most of what You had said. You said in the video that if You want someone to hear they will hear, otherwise sound waves reach everyone's ears. Who is it that truly hears, truly sees, truly knows? Agha Jan, You said, everyone speaks of Rumi's love for Shams, but people do not realize that it was Shams who planted the seed in Rumi's heart for that love to blossom, for Rumi to be Rumi. You said, in other words, what Rumi was seeing was his own true self that resides within and that was Shams' masterful skill. Agha Jan, I think the VCR industry is certainly taking the harvest of all this. Everyone is glued to their set each chance they get to watch and absorb. You also said, books, tapes, etc., do not bear the necessities of the growth that the Teacher's Presence imparts. But we have two hours of Your precious teachings that answers and unfolds so many unknowns for the human race. So much You've said that will set scientists and scholars right on their paths of discoveries. You've opened the door of Knowledge, but I can tell from the shadow of sadness on Your Face that what You've revealed will only be used by mankind to exploit and rule and not for the cultivation of human dignity, peace and survival. What a pity, Agha Jan.

Agha Jan, my trip to Thailand was indeed interesting...especially the event about the dead person's soul rising. I cried and asked You to intercede, to help him. His wife, family and friends were gathered, a whole battalion of monks were scheduled for each day to perform the rituals for his soul. The monks were absorbed in their chants, and everyone attentively observed the rituals, yet no one could see and hear how he was suffering, how he was shrieking with pain; no one could see him outside the coffin. So many wreaths were sent by the royal family, by all the dignitaries expressing their grief for such a unique and truly good man. Yes, no one could see or hear him. I started crying and asked You and Your Beloved Father to help him. I said our Holy Prayer so many times. After the ceremony my friend asked why I was crying. I told her. She was dumfounded and presented the case to her husband, who was reluctant to say anything to the aunts for they would never be open to such a statement. But, I kept praying for him at prayer times, at meditation times and in between. Finally, on the Sunday where everyone had gathered for extra special prayers, one of the aunts told my friend that she had dreamt of her brother asking for help and had asked for special services to be conducted in English. The aunt had interpreted that to mean to hold services at a church. My friend told her about what I had seen. So, with much skepticism which was veiled with politeness and courtesy, they asked me to hold a special meditation service, where that very fine aunt was to be present. I could feel her true desire for his freedom and survival as she entered the room. I asked everyone to sit in a circle and prepared them to be present and began with the Holy Prayer. Then we proceeded with the services, and I read the passage from *The Secret Word*:

For the Forty Guiding Lanterns of Sufism,
Guide the Child of Fate to the Predestined Goal.

And remove the leaves of death from the branches of life,
And by the truth of Divine and everlasting knowledge,
By the truth of the awareness in the elevated Mountain of Ghaf,
Clear the dust of shadows from the illumined face,
And reveal the identity.
Time has arrived,
The talisman and boundaries of time are broken,
Place is interlaced,
An unlimited tremor demolished the boundaries,
All things from every direction became united,
And the endless heavens are adorned by the dawn of truth,
And the ancient song by Venus was played.
Through the vastness of heavens there was nothing but the truth,
Neither Eastern nor Western,
And at the summit of the skies,
And at the cleavage of the horizons,
And the Crescent of Oneness,
The Father's call summons the child....

As I read this I could see You taking him and moving him on and tears swelled up in my eyes, but I read on and witnessed his journey. Agha Jan, does this mean that he must have done something right to have received such a blessing? Imagine, for me to have gone to Thailand at such time and ...Or was it a sign for the family and friends to realize that this is the Path to the everlasting life?

At the end of the services I told the gathering that one of them will receive a message from him that he is well. That very aunt dreamt of him that night and he had thanked her.

But Agha Jan, they have forgotten. Their lives go on as before, and they did not stop to think what would happen to them when they will die. Perhaps the lesson to be learned is most of all for me.

Something special did take place during this trip. I met a lovely Thai family, well educated, successful, kind, and wonderful parents. Their daughter is so cute, she squeaks with joy at the attention she gets and the boy acts mature to show he is the older of the two. I sent their photographs for You, so they would be blessed by You. We've been in touch through these months; she wanted to continue with her skills in meditation. One day she called me, distraught, about her father who'd been hospitalized with a bad case of cancer. I tried to comfort her and gave her hope that I'd try to ask for Your guidance and prayers. It's interesting, as soon as I said this, she calmed down. We've been on the phone frequently these past two months. I spoke with her the other day, and she said she was going on a trip and suddenly had felt afraid of the airplane. So she began to say the Holy Prayer, but realized that she'd forgotten to take the text with her. She recited from memory, but as soon as she got to her hotel she called her office and the prayer was faxed over to her, so she'd be sure she wouldn't make a mistake.

Agha Jan, when more people discover the magic of our Holy Prayer, I wouldn't be surprised if all countries changed their national anthem to our Holy Prayer.

Agha Jan, thank You for Your blessings. The Holy month of Ramazan ended and I was in perfect health. It was different this year than the previous years. It was heavy and the load of the body was difficult to bear. The previous years were light and transparent. However, the effects are now appearing. Last night as I was preparing for my midnight vigil, it suddenly flashed in my heart that if I have no desires, whatever it is that I need, You will give me. It was a strange feeling. I feel You are within me—it is You—I just have to stop doing from habit whatever it is that I do. Agha Jan, when I first started reading the Holy Book, Your Beloved Father speaks of the **source of life** in the heart, I knew it was a reference to God. Now I have experienced it. I keep coming across experiences realizing that You are witness to whatever I do, and direct what I do. I recall many years ago when we had come to Your House, You said, I'm a stranger in My own House. I knew it had many layers of meaning. One of them being–the heart is the House of God, and humans are ignorant of the presence of God within their hearts. It has been Your guidance and blessings that I have come to such realization, so how can I ask You to give me more, when You have given without my asking? Agha Jan, You always give without our asking. Agha Jan, from deep within my heart I have been praying for the closeness that I used to experience. It is starting to come back now—Your Presence—the translucency, the fineness, the loveliness, just everything that Your Presence brings.

Agha Jan, many Ramazan's ago, I sent You this poem that I had written to send to a scholar:

> From the deep corners of my heart
> A long awaited wish crystallized
> As I read your endearing praise
> Of your friend, Massignon.
> Seven years I've spent with my Beloved's Face
> From dawn to dusk, an unbroken chain
> His love, His constant penetrating gaze
> Gently transforming my blatant earthly self
> With the fire of love He instilled within my heart
> Seeking venues to chant, to celebrate His love
> Yet, crippled I am, barren, without tools
> To sing His praise
> So, upon reading your words
> Massignon's self and soul
> Mirrored by Hallaj's faith and love
> Wedded with your passion for Gilgamesh
> Brought my heart's pleas before my precious God
> I explained my encounter with you
> Your skill—a life-time of labor, study and

All else unknown to me,
Of Massignon's constant inquiries,
Studies, scholarship
All the tools and talent you both possess
To celebrate your loved one's praise
So, I beseeched my God
You, who have blessed me to love You
So tenderly
And, unveiled Your Face—
The Water of eternal Life
The pearl of youth
The joy of paradise
The essence of ruby wine
You, who can will anything
To be
Bless me with the gift
To selflessly sing Your praise—
The love my heart knows so well
Grant me the words, the talent
Or, the purity my soul needs
To be in harmony with You
To sing
To be Your parakeet
For I have no scholarship
Nor wealth of words
But I long to sing
My love for You.

Agha Jan, You surprised me again. You scolded me so severely that I felt like an orphan again. You said, don't you know I despise superstition and the like? Don't you know that water must first stir before it comes to a boil? How often have I told You, I despise beggars.

You must earn your bread! Agha Jan, it was Ramazan and I was totally heart broken. My eyes were so swollen from the tears they poured out that I had to hang onto the walls to find my whereabouts.

Agha Jan, this was four years ago. I guess I must have reached the scolding age. Infants are not scolded but children certainly are. Well, that scolding wasn't the last, my eyes bear witness to it. I remember, a few years ago, You gave me the worst possible scolding. The four star general had told You a tale to put things in her favor and make me look like a genuine monster. That's what I assumed had happened from the scolding You gave me—the slightest hint that I've displeased You just devastates me. While You were speaking to me, I was choking from dismay. I fell down into a deep coma, which lasted for many days. Each time I'd open my eyes I'd feel that I'd truly been betrayed. Little did I know that the lesson at hand was for me to learn to turn the other cheek, and respect my elders, especially if they're sickly and frail. All the while I was thinking, if I can't trust Agha Jan to know the real truth, whom can I trust?

Agha Jan, I used to be so infuriated when I'd see these sly thieves sneak into our gatherings to steal Your teachings and market them as their own. One of them tried to swoon me off my feet, and take me to their House of Justice to teach. Little did he know that it'd be himself who'd be smitten with love, falling at Your Feet. Agha Jan, Your ways never cease to amaze me!

Agha Jan, once when I was sitting before You, You gave an example of a musical instrument. You said, who knows the true value of a violin, the master musician or the fickle child? It's the musician who knows how to extract the best notes, while the child scratches your ears and the violin. Later, you'll see that the child's violin has ended up in the garbage bin, while the musician's stands shining on the mantle piece. It's your choice, do you want to be played by the master musician, or end up in the garbage bin?

Agha Jan, You said, value yourself. What is the tune that you must display, how do you know what tune to display? Is it the violin that plays, or is it the master's hand that brings out the most magnificent tunes from the silence of the wood and strings?

Agha Jan, I remember being told that during the journey's last folds, You give your children a special word which they ceaselessly say to take them through their last steps to You. This must be that invisible rope that connects to the Almighty Lord. Agha Jan, is there another word that would connect Your children to You, but Your Name?

Agha Jan, is it true that the siblings whom You allow to discard their shells, You allow to help the toddlers along? They too must be the unseen angels of Your Soul, Agha Jan. I wish You'd send a highly skilled one to help me along with the translations.

Agha Jan, when I watch newborn infants, I often wonder what goes on behind the motion of their eyes and the smile on their lips. It seems they must be dreaming. But they haven't had any accessible memory files from which to draw dreams, nor do they yet need to daydream. So it must be that their soul is still in tune with their true home. I wonder what they're seeing that we can't see. I often hear the children of the siblings say, "Look, Agha Jan's right here." When the grown ups look up, they can't see You. But the children say, "Agha Jan just tickled me under my chin, or squeezed my cheek, or patted me on the head." Well, Agha Jan, these children don't have to work hard like us, they don't have to search a lifetime to see God. Besides, their parents have been cleansed, so their genes are rare. So, these children can see and hear You, when others don't.

Agha Jan, at one of our Sunday gatherings, one of the older siblings told us that Delilah symbolized the unruly "self," while Samson stood for the heavenly "self." The seven strands of hair that Delilah cut were Samson's connection to the heavenly kingdom. When Samson forgot his Father and his home, his strength gave way, for he had lost the connection, since each strand of hair was connected to one of the heavens through which each human must ascend. Agha Jan, he made sure to tell us that those were Your words, he knew we wouldn't believe it if it came from him.

Agha Jan, if Eden is paradise, does it mean that when humans get engaged solely with their senses, that's when they're cast out of Eden? Is that how we lose memory of our true home, while infants still see the dominions of God?

Agha Jan, I don't want to be like anyone but You—I want to be more than 24 karat gold. Agha Jan, why can't world leaders, scientists, politicians, etc., simply admit that they don't know and need to know? Why don't they come to You? Their problem is they think they know. They don't stop to think that if they knew, the current state of the world wouldn't be such a catastrophe. People are awarded for "peace," for "human rights," for "economics," etc., and where do we see peace, human rights, equal opportunity, equal living conditions, and equality? Shouldn't this be a statement? Why do these leaders get so much pay, when they don't know how to make things right? Sane people don't keep going to the same doctor when they keep getting worse. Are they put in position and power because they don't know, or because they know how to make a mess of things and confuse the public?

Agha Jan, You've always said, isn't it crucial first to know the human being before you can do any sound planning? You said in Your Holy Book that when the spaceship was sent up a figure of a man and woman was drawn on the spaceship; this is how humans know themselves. Their identity is their physical existence. You've declared that it is the recognition of the truth of the human being in his or her heavenly realm which results in more constant and correct laws. Agha Jan, no one is listening, no one hears!

Agha Jan, I usually watch this late evening program where supposedly the mightiest of "intellectual, economic, political and social minds" are brought to present their views. It's so sad, it reminds me of what one reads about in the time of the gladiators. They are thrown at each other, and each makes a perfect defense—so convincing. How can two people present such opposing views on the same topic so convincingly? Do they hear the facts differently, or do they want us to think that we've heard them differently? But all in all, no one knows what they're up to and what really goes on behind the scenes. Only You know, Agha Jan. Just last week when You were explaining to the woman from Asia about injustice, You said, is Africa worse than the Sinai desert for cultivation and harvest? It's to the advantage of those in control to keep others poor so they can rule. If such wonderful oranges can be cultivated in the desert in Israel, can't the same be done in Africa? So, think before you accuse God of injustice and human strife. It's human greed which brings about suffering. The rich don't give the rich free rides, it's the poor who provide the free rides.

Agha Jan, in Your book *Peace* You have said everything. Those who are shrewd have taken Your words and use them to speak eloquently, while continuing the strife against the weak and needy. Agha Jan, it's so very sad.

Agha Jan, as I was driving back from the Khaneghah tonight, I thought that the American police can be cruel and violent because of prejudice and bias. I pursued this thought. The violence, greed, and ugliness is passed down—generation to generation—so that the culture breeds these traits. Then I recalled, You have taught us that nothing leaves the universe. Nothing can be added to or deducted from the universe. So, all the attributes we bear, all of our actions and their effects, are handed down. Then I thought, what hope is there for humanity? So You gave me the answer, it is true that nothing can be added or deducted, but things can be transformed. It is transformation—the science of alchemy—Your knowledge, that can save humanity alone and break the vicious impregnable wall of human vice. Agha Jan, is this the meaning of the words of Your Beloved Father, in the *Message from the Soul*, "Do not rebel so much that you be abandoned on earth because of your sins; the lives of your children may yet be your redemption." Agha Jan, ever since I asked You about the meaning of this sentence, eight years ago, You have been opening my eyes so that

I may experience the meaning behind the words. I understand that "children" does not necessarily mean physical children that we bear, but it is the result of the true repentance that comes from knowing God. When that repentance occurs, then our actions are our children, and they will be done according to Your will, and they will be nourished by sustenance from Your Hand, and thus they will be our redemption. Thank You, Agha Jan.

Agha Jan, it's so difficult to be among people who haven't been trained by You. Some are like savages. It's painful to be among them. I think my armor is no longer protecting me. My tolerance for their ignorance and arrogance, and worse of all their savagery, is really at a breaking point. Agha Jan, it's ever more difficult. The law of the flesh rules them and overpowers any urge to seek the sublime. How can I speak about Your words, when people think knowing themselves is time consuming? After all, running after money, position, power, and lust are more important to them. No one has time to stop and discover the knowledge imbedded in this exquisite piece of machinery—the human body—and to find out how it really works. I remember once You said, do you buy a T.V. set and use it as a table for your flower pot? Do you buy an electric stove and use it as a dining table? When do you want to learn what the purpose of your body is? Agha Jan, people tell me, if you don't drink, if you don't do this or that, that's not living! I guess suicide to them probably is slitting the wrist, hanging one's self, or other violent means. Can any intelligent person, if honest and sincere, admit that drinking brings clarity and sharpness of mind?

I remember the words of Your Beloved Father, "How can you live in the same place as a rotten corpse?" When people can't really live with themselves, they turn to things that hush their awareness and their agitated state, so the agony is muffled for awhile. When the effect is gone they go back to their deals and ordeals, and so the world goes on.

Agha Jan, the ignorant and foolish always say that the Sufis were the lovers of women and wine. If they'd use one of their brain cells, they'd know that it is impossible for such majestic work to be produced under the influence of wine. They do not know that the Beloved is You, the wine is the love You pour in our hearts referred to as the cup. Didn't they kill Jesus because he said he was the son of God? Didn't they hang Hallaj for having said, "I am God?" He was the true Moslem, for he tore down the veil of duality between himself and God and attested to the oneness of God. All these people who run around and call themselves Moslems, in every prayer they say, there is no other but God. If they attest to it, then their action must bear testimony to it. It's easy enough to see that they're far from it. Are they All-Knowing, are they All-Seeing, are they....? After all, if one is annihilated in God, only God manifests through him. Agha Jan, they are so ignorant that they don't even know they're lying. You said, if God is absolute, then how can anything but Him exist. If you say God exists here and you exist there, then you have to change the definition of absolute. Agha Jan, You always teach us how to tear down the veils, to truly the oneness declare.

Agha Jan, Your Beloved Father has said in His book *The Epic of Existence*, "The truth of Islam will be revealed in....years." The truth of Islam is *la-elaha-ella-Allah*—there is no other but God. Agha Jan, that time is nearing, does that mean that You will reveal Your identity by that year to humanity?

Agha Jan, is it correct to deduce that those who want the world are Jews, those who want the heavens are Christians, and those who strive for oneness with God are Moslems? You've always taught us to put our worldly life and actions in order first, then discover about the heaven within our hearts, and journey on the way to oneness with God. You've told us so many times, don't get stuck but move on. So, to be a Moslem, we must first be a Jew and then a Christian.

Agha Jan, I think I finally know the meaning of, "God guides those, whom He wills." After so many years of thinking about it, the answer just flashed in my head. It's so obvious now. The key word is guidance. What does guidance mean? It means God reveals Himself to whom-ever He wants. It's simple. How can it be otherwise? In day-to-day friendships humans choose with whom they want to associate, have for friends, or to love. After all, why should God not choose whom He wishes to know Him? So, He places the urge in the hearts of those whom He wants to know Him. Those in whom the urge is not, simply think those who search for God are foolish. So where is the injustice in this? After all, doesn't everything return to its Origin? It's true, they are Your words, "Everything returns to its Origin." Is it possible to search for something that has never existed, doesn't exist and will never exist? If it's possible, then it's beyond me. I just recalled Your Beloved Father's words in the *Manifestations of Thought*, "Man, in his own truth, can perceive a perfect specimen of everything which is found in the universe." We essentially search for what exists, because the urge to search comes from that sample which exists within. So, we start the search for what we have within from the outside. In the same manner, when we search for God, we think we have to go somewhere and do some extraordinary thing. Haven't all of Your Holy Ancestry said, "*La-elaha-ella-Allah*." And hasn't it been said centuries ago, "If you break the heart of each particle, a hundred pure seas shall come of it. There came a hundred heaps inside a grain, then came a world in the heart of a millet." So, Agha Jan, where is it that You are not?

Agha Jan, once when I was really frustrated because everyone kept saying there are many ways to God, You said, tell them if you want to go to San Francisco, will the road to Miami take you there? How many ways of eating are there? There's only one way, and that's through the mouth. You said, the fork, the plate and napkin are not breakfast, lunch and dinner, you must have the food so your hunger can be satisfied. You may keep staring at your plate, or keep lifting the empty fork to your mouth, but it doesn't give the nutrient your body needs for survival. People keep talking about different paths but are they getting what they need for their survival beyond this physical form?

Agha Jan, I remember an example You gave once that really cleared many questions for me. You said, you don't see drivers in cars that have been taken to the junk yard. When the cars are being compressed for recycling the drivers aren't allowed to be in them. If the driver is attached to his car, he will stand by in pain and watch what's happening to his car. The same holds true for you. If all you know of yourself is this machine, then you'll be in pain. Don't forget, you're not the machine. So, know yourself before the machine's time is up!

Agha Jan, You've said, the sky and the mountains cannot contain Me, but the heart of the believer is My dwelling place. Agha Jan, please make my heart Your dwelling place always. You've said in Your book *The Approaching Promise*, "Through intricate labyrinths revolves the way to the hidden secrets of heart." Is this the secret of the Journey— ultimately attaining oneness with You, as symbolically told in *The Conference of the Birds*—the beautiful allegory by Sheikh Attar? You've said also in this Book, "To your soul He will reveal the precious essence of this secret." Agha Jan, You are the precious Secret, so very precious. My heart cannot be contained, it leaps at the word "precious," Agha Jan. You are so very precious. O' Generous One, O' Compassionate and Merciful. Agha Jan, isn't it time for everyone to know You? My throat is so tight from the love surging from my heart. My body is too frail to endure the awe of beholding You.

Agha Jan, it's beautiful to see how our circle has grown. All the new siblings! Each so joyous at witnessing the miracles in their lives. They have such lustrous tears in their eyes when they speak Your Name, Agha Jan. As they speak of You with such love, my heart sends that electricity through every fiber of my being, and uncontrollable tears just pour down my face. Agha Jan, You've set in motion the lightning and the entire world is catching the fire of Your Love. This must be the resurrection! Souls coming to life in the dark tomb of the body. Is the day of judgment now, Agha Jan?

Agha Jan, You once said that Mecca is situated at the most potent magnetic center of the Earth. You said, God knows where to erect His House! Agha Jan, then is the heart of the believer—Your House—the most potent magnetic center as well? That's why You've said the **source of life** resides in the heart. Your Beloved Father has said in the *Message from the Soul*, "Gather all the strength that is spread in your senses and body, concentrate and calm them in your heart at night, and manifest your luminous figure. If life is given to you by the **source of life** in your heart, you will not be subject to death."

Agha Jan, does the moth know that the candle flame will claim its life? Often, I wish that I had the same urge, perseverance and courage. To be consumed, what bliss! The moth doesn't stop circling the candle flame. Agha Jan, humans have been given the brain and the power of reason to look at the marvels of nature and the universe and ask, what is it all about? I suppose those who don't give up the search, ultimately end up before You! Reason seeks Knowledge until it is finally satisfied. Everything that You have given a sample of to mankind, You have all of it in its absolute form. So, everything has to come back to You. We search for beauty, and our need for beauty is fulfilled when we behold You. We search for love, and our desire for love is satisfied when You love us. We search for kindness, generosity, compassion, benevolence, etc., and in beholding You, our thirst is quenched. You have placed samples of it all within our souls, so we seek and ultimately find You. So, everything must return to its Origin. No wonder it's so hard to keep everyone away from You. Agha Jan, free my soul, so I can always be with You.

Agha Jan, Agha Jan, You must have really spoiled me well on this last trip and never ever let me know it while I was in Your Presence. You didn't even glance at me, and never uttered a word, except to motion me where to sit and ask if everyone who was to be there was present.

Agha Jan, You responded to everyone's questions with much patience, and You healed and blessed them. You gave us so many jewels of wisdom. You spoke of helping and healing the abused, the addicted and the needy. The social scientists were baffled by Your knowledge, and they'd only witnessed but a millionth of one drop.

Agha Jan, someone asked You to explain about the reality of life. You said, when you say reality of life you are creating boundaries of language and human thought to define reality. Reality is absolute. Life is absolute. Then, You explained how people create boundaries in defining themselves. You said Life and living are different. You said, you have to experience "Reality" to know what reality is, you have to experience "Life" to know what life is. Otherwise, for each word used to define them, your brain will quickly draw up its own images.

Agha Jan, then someone asked You about addictions. You said, to resolve any problem you must discover the reason for the behavior. When the person realizes the source of the problem then he can do something about it. If he has been physically punished for doing something at a certain age, he will repeat the same behavior when he grows. Now he drinks and ruins his stomach, or takes drugs, etc., and ruins his system. He doesn't realize that his body has done nothing wrong to be punished for it now. He must first realize what he is doing, then he can do something about it. If in the past you have had unfulfilled things in your life, you can't make up for them now. You said, you must realize that time is gone and now it's the time to do something else. People always want to recreate things from the past, in the hope of getting the fulfillment now. That's the reason for many of the addictions and problems.

Agha Jan, someone asked You about religious wars. You said, didn't the North Koreans fight the South Koreans, didn't the North Vietnamese and the South Vietnamese fight each other? When a cow is branded on its tail showing which farm it belongs to, does that mean the cow is not a cow? When you look at a flower, do you look at its petals, color, leaves, etc., or at its beauty, the presence it has? Are you a human being or a Thai? Above anything else you are a human being. If you realize that you are a human being first, then where can differences come from? Religion and culture have been used for exploiting people for money and power.

Agha Jan, then the scholar who had studied Your book *Peace* asked what You meant by, "All revolutions devour their own children" and why You had made the statement? You said, it's very clear, all you need to do is to look at history. Haven't all revolutions supposedly wanted to bring better conditions for the people? But, we see that after awhile corruption sets in. The best way to understand this is to look at what happens when a germ invades the body. Usually, antibiotics are prescribed under such circumstances. It doesn't take long before the germ changes its "killer" into foodstuff for itself. Then another antibiotic is prescribed to combat it. And so it goes on. Make the system strong to uproot the germ so health will be maintained. The same holds true for revolutions which aspire to change human conditions. First, the human being must be fully known. Everyone fails to see that greed, power, and such things are not injected from the outside. Each human being bears all the heritage of his ancestry and all that has gone before them, now what is the antibiotic that will combat all these germs? Then, You gave him Your Book *Peace* and told him to read the following passages:

> *Devising any compulsory system which forces human beings into a predefined structure not in harmony with the nature of the human being will result in explosion and devastation.*

> *Only laws and social systems which are not rationally and scientifically opposed to the essence of the human being will be permanent and enforceable.*

> *A prosperous human society is attained through the outward and inward harmony of each of its members, and their harmonious existence in a unified system.*

> *The true meaning of peace refers to the inner freedom and spiritual elevation of every individual. The intention of the Holy Prophets has been to educate humanity to reach the true essence of the human being. Unless this dimension in each person is uncovered and brought to the fore, true peace and human rights will not be realized.*

Agha Jan, then You added very soothingly and quietly, ask God to show you the One whose Hand heals mankind's pain. There was a long silence after this. Thank You for the prayer, Agha Jan.

Agha Jan, then someone asked You why there is so much abuse against women in the Holy Book. You said, people don't give themselves permission to pick up a physics book and criticize it when they don't know physics. What does an illiterate person know of physics? Will you listen to his judgments, comments, recommendations? Why do you think that the Holy Book revealed by God to His Prophet is less significant and does not require its own knowledge for its truth to be known? You must first know what is meant by "woman" before accusing God of abuse.

Agha Jan, then someone asked You, why there's suffering, why her father had suffered so much? You said, what gives you the right to judge? If your father was suffering, were you experiencing the same pain? Or, was it because of your attachments to him, all those years that those attachments had developed, and the fear of him no longer being with you? What made you suffer, did you really feel his pain? How often have you thought of him since he died, as much as when he was alive? You said, the most Holy Lord of believers has said, to be a judge you have to know what is on this side and what is on that side. How can you be the judge when you don't have knowledge of the entire picture?

Agha Jan, then someone asked You if the soul existed. You said, how much air is in this room? She said, a lot. You stretched out Your arm, and said, is there air where my hand is? She said yes. Then, You said, if I take my hand away, does it mean there is no air, just because my hand is not there? The spirit is absolute, the body is like the hand.

Agha Jan, then someone asked You about the disciples of Christ and Buddha. You said, they had followers and not disciples. There's a great deal of difference between a follower and a disciple. People may follow you for various motivations, but a disciple's sole goal is to learn what the teacher knows. Now tell me, did Jesus or Buddha train someone to be just like them?

Agha Jan, the key to Your teachings that day was faith upon which stand hope and respect, and upon them health rests. You said, teach people to have respect, teach them to be independent and don't make beggars out of people. People react to the circumstances of those in need through their own emotional lens. They say, let's give this child three meals a day since he gets food only every 12 hours. They don't realize that the child's system has adapted itself to having less food. They give him three meals a day and make him dependent on three meals a day. Tell me, when they're gone who's going to feed that child? You said, take yourself out of the picture and see what they really need.

Agha Jan, You said people give food, clothing, etc., to those in need, thinking they've taken care of the pain. Did they know what their pain was—their pain is still there. If they haven't experienced the same pain, they don't know what those in pain are saying. Others give money to the poor, how do they know that money's not going to be used on drugs, etc.? How do you know what you're giving them is not going to kill them? Agha Jan, You said the rich and the poor both have pain. The rich have the material things to cover their pain. The rich have someone to talk to, they have food, shelter, etc., but they still have the pain. So where is it that you should look for relief and release? Talking to someone helps, but for how long? How can you fulfill people's needs when they don't know what their needs are? You adopt a child thinking you're going to give him a better life. What guarantee do you have that at the age of 18 he'll not have the social ills of your society? You said, don't misunderstand me, I don't mean don't help anyone, but be aware of what you are doing.

Agha Jan, You said, but it's best to be healthy, then speak of health. So, become perfect and then help others. Agha Jan, how can anyone be perfect but You? No wonder it's only You who takes care of whomever is in need.

I recalled a statement You had made a long time ago. Agha Jan, I said, everyone thinks it's impossible for peace to prevail and human strife to end and they don't believe me when I say, it's possible if everyone's trained. They always say, how can such a thing take place? You said, tell them, does it take more than a lit match stick to put an entire forest afire?

Agha Jan, I think my brain fuse popped, since I don't recall the rest of Your words. But I do recall that You emphasized another point. You said, by what do you measure anything? If you want to compare if my hair is more black than hers, what is the standard by which you can determine? For any comparison you need a constant standard, then you can give value to the rest.

Well, after I left with the delegation who had come from all over the world to have an audience with You, and after I saw them off, I just crawled into my brittle shell and cried and cried. These weren't the usual tears, but tears from my heart. It's true, I tasted them, and they were sweet! Agha Jan, I felt so totally abandoned. I said to myself, why are you such a fool, when will you ever learn, Agha Jan doesn't give a hoot about you, when will you learn? I must have passed out from sadness that night. I couldn't even bring myself to say prayers. How could I have prayed, when I said God simply doesn't care? Anyway, the next morning I got up and cleansed myself inside and out and said, I'll go for a walk since I have all day. It was a perfect Spring day, and I was staying at a dismal hotel next to the airport. But as I walked out and started discovering my whereabouts, I saw the ocean, and walking over, I saw such beautiful flowers—yellows, creams, fuchsias—all wild and glimmering in their naked beauty. I just kept walking on, unable to control my tears. And these words I sung for You, Agha Jan:

> There are no Eyes into which
> my soul can freely fly,
> The pearls of my eyes
> the rubies and sapphires
> are the tears of my soul
> that longs for Your Eyes,
> There are no Eyes into which

my soul can freely fly
You said, faith is the key
  to hope and respect
  with hope and respect
  you'll have health
  and all the rest,
But, how can I have
  faith, hope and respect
  when Your Eyes are now veiled
  and my soul has no resting place?
There are no Eyes into which
  my soul can freely fly,
The pearls of my eyes
  the rubies and sapphires
  will await a glance from Your smile
  so my soul will have faith,
  hope and respect,
But till then,
  the pearls of my eyes
  the rubies and sapphires
  will keep the memories
  of Your Eyes into which
  my soul once freely flew
But till then,
  where is faith,
  so I can have
  hope and respect
  and be healed
  of the past
  and be released
  of future fears
But till then,
But till then...

> The pearls of my eyes
> the rubies and sapphires....

So I hummed and hummed and tears flowed and flowed until I was completely empty. I wonder if it was all Your doing, Agha Jan. I was to be ready at 4 p.m. so I could be in Your Presence by 5 o'clock that afternoon. It is Your Beloved Father's words, "Don't enter the House of God uncleansed." I truly felt empty. We entered Your House at 5 p.m. sharp. The siblings who had driven me said, no matter what time we leave to go to Agha Jan's House, we always arrive at 5 o'clock sharp! I thought I was totally numb from the past hours, but my heart quickly let me know that what needed to be awake was quite alert. This time I didn't try to stare down the door until You'd come. I simply closed my eyes and went inside. Suddenly I felt a swift motion of energy and I was pulled up. You were entering. I suppose everyone else had been staring down the door, so they were all up in a flash, and I guess I was pulled up too.

I had heard from one of the siblings that the students in Your private class say the Holy Prayer in one breath. At least I was mentally prepared, but I had to gasp for breath very quickly. Then the Holy Koran was so beautifully sung by the student whom everyone considers one of the "favorites." Well, of course they have to sparkle if they are in the presence of the Sun every week, endlessly. I guess they must be the sunflowers and we must be the ivy.

But Agha Jan, I've never heard You speak so. There was no break, no pause, no past, no future, nor anything ever heard before in the words You spoke. It was Existence manifest through eloquence. I said to myself after You paused, I'm so far behind. I don't even understand what Agha Jan says anymore. But later I realized that the first few moments in which You swept us through eternity was the kernel of what was to unfold in the coming four hours.

I recall when You first began to speak Your Face was drawn. But as You spoke Your Face returned to its ever illuminating glow. Every cell in my body was recording Your words. I had told myself I must concentrate on Your words and not be captivated by Your beauty. I must have been absorbed totally, I never felt my feet or legs this time, except when we were told to leave. My feet couldn't be turned straight again even hours after I had left Your Presence. Thank You, Agha Jan.

Agha Jan, one of the siblings told me something a few days later that made my heart flutter and flutter with joy. She said, after the Holy *Zekr* (chant of remembrance,) when the lights were faintly turned on and everyone was still, You looked at me for about five minutes. I thought, how could that be possible, one minute is an eternity, let alone five. I remember I raised my head once when the Holy *Zekr* was over and saw that Your Head was slightly bent and Your Hand was on Your Forehead as if shading Your Eyes from the sun. So, I quickly lowered my eyes and didn't look up again, since I didn't want to intrude on Your privacy. But how blessed I am...five entire minutes!

Agha Jan, during the Holy *Zekr* my body took over with the motions of my heart and so did my voice, but my brain wasn't dead! A few days later I began to write to You and ask You to truly reveal to me even once what true *Zekr* is really about. That same night at midnight You took over and my body started spinning in the motion of the Holy *Zekr* and within I was truly illuminated. I realized what it meant to be empty of self and be filled with God. The boundaries of the self had disappeared and only You remained. It was a totally new feeling which persisted for a few days. I realized that in this state there is no human error. This must be the state of those who attain annihilation in God. It was the most peaceful and undisturbed state. It's so difficult to describe it. It happened just that once. I wish I had asked You for it to be continuous. Agha Jan, will You grant me this state?

Agha Jan, on this blessed evening You said, for any action, idea, etc., to be manifest it must be founded upon a stable principle. However, with the passage of time and because of individual tastes, weaknesses, likes, and dislikes, people start deviating from that principle. Humans usually keep close to principles that give them tangible benefits.

For example, to construct buildings humans keep the principles since they need them. If matters do not require immediate results, the search for their origin is less immediate. What I understood from Your words was this: if humans feel a need for survival they look for the source so they can build on a solid foundation for their survival. Humans do this for their physical needs because those are evident, but when it comes to going beyond physical needs they don't go to the Source but accept through hearsay or depend on their own thoughts, or simply negate them. How can human thought that changes so much give constant, unchanging results? Humans search to find stable laws to meet their physical needs, but when it comes to religion, superstition and blind obedience take over.

You said, return to the Origin in religion is called repentance and it's for those for whom knowing God is as urgent as their daily bread. Those looking for true repentance are few in number, and they are the ones who are truly "research-oriented." Some use the Holy Book as an oracle. Tell me, who in his right mind would consult a physics book to decide whether to get married, write a contract, take a trip, or when to retire? People use the Holy Book in such dark-age ways, no wonder their ignorance is passed down from generation to generation. They call God to pay their debts, to win a lottery ticket, to get to work on time, to heal their ills. Even if all your needs are met, are you stabilized in the constant and permanent law for your life now, and are you assured of your existence in the hereafter to be without flaw?

You said, since people don't search for the Origin but simply accept what they're fed, they live in a state of turmoil; they have no stable roots to hold them in place.

You said, return to the **source of life** in your heart where the true Teacher is introduced by God. The brain is then submitted to the heart and is able to know all things as they truly are. You said, the power of the heart fuels the grey area of the brain to expand its field and move beyond physical laws. To make stable discoveries, to know things beyond the shadow of a doubt, to become stable and pure, return to your Origin, become purified and stabilized so you'll know who you truly are. It's this Teacher who can take you on the journey of your soul, that your brain knows nothing about.

You said, when a child is told to take a glass of water and drink it, the child doesn't analyze but does it, so his thirst is quenched. Humans say they want their thirst to be quenched but instead of picking up the glass and drinking it, they analyze the process and try to figure out what it would be like if they drank the water. Agha Jan, no wonder everyone's dying of thirst. Agha Jan, You said, how can absolute laws be known through limited unstable inputs of the brain? You said, if you're sincere in your search for God, sit and confess your need in earnest, wait in the darkness of your heart and ask Him to reveal Himself to you, and save you from yourself.

You said, the Holy Prophet who first said, "He is God, the One and Only," was there, had the experience, then voiced His experience. But people keep repeating these words, not realizing how vain it is to repeat the words without the experience. Agha Jan, then You gave us the secret of creation with a brisk statement. You said, when a drop is in the ocean, does it know the majesty of the ocean? I didn't know what to say, because I had read in Your Beloved Father's books, "When the drop returns to the ocean, it's no longer the drop but the ocean." As soon as this thought crossed my mind You said, no! The drop must be separated from the ocean to see how small it is before the ocean, then it knows the majesty of the ocean. How swiftly You covered the mystery of creation! You left our brains gasping for air, as You spoke on. You said, in order to discover anything beyond the physical, total purification is a necessity. Ask God to show you the one whose Hand heals and whose Breath imparts eternal life.

You said, you don't have to go far to know God's laws. Isn't the earth the offspring of the sun? See how it revolves and revolves around the sun? When it revolves around itself, the side away from the sun in darkness remains. The side facing the sun is nourished from the sun. Repentance is the same. When your face is turned towards God, darkness is dissolved. Repentance doesn't mean to seek forgiveness when you think you've done something wrong. True repentance comes about when a soul has searched and searched and finally recognized God. Now his face is turned towards the ever illuminating Sun. Now, if he turns away from the Sun, it's his own death that he brings about. No harm is done to the Sun. The Sun's there to shine and shine, no matter if you face it or not. So, look within and see what it is that you want.

You said, everything in the universe is infinite and that is the law! Just observe your thoughts. As soon as you allow your thoughts to roam, see how far they go. Humans consider their birth date as their point of origin, and begin to count their days from their departure from the womb. They don't even count the nine months and nine days that the fetus was in the womb. How can they even want to go beyond this and realize that life just didn't happen then, but has had an infinite journey and the earth is just a stopping place.

You said, have you ever heard the sound of an apple turning red or the sound of a flower opening? You said, your hearing and sight is also infinite, but awareness of your capacity is so limited.

You said, the earth is absorbed by the sun, and the sun is absorbed by another sun, and so on. At this point I realized that ultimately everything is on its journey of absorption by You. I recall Your Beloved Father's words in *The Epic of Existence*:

> *All is all, together or alone,*
> *All by all, silently hum the call.*

You said, you existed yesterday, you exist today, in sleep you exist, when dreaming you exist, when you eat you exist, so when is it that you are not?

You said, if you turn the T.V. off it doesn't mean that the station doesn't exist or the program is not there. All that exists in the universe is within you. It's you who's turned the machinery off.

You said, don't forget, a prisoner in a cell needs someone who's not in prison to get him out of jail. So, who do you know who's free and can free you from the prison of your earthly shell?

Agha Jan, You had been holding a piece of metal in Your hand, and You said, this iron has more flexibility than you. When I give it energy it bends, I don't see the same in humans. When you come here, some things happen for you, discoveries take place, and you think it's your own doing. When you leave you go back to your own customs and habits and you behave as before.

You said, I am at the peak of this mountain and you are at the bottom. Come up to where I am so you too will have faith. You are like the followers of Moses, with all the miracles you've seen you'll end up worshipping a calf. Do you know why they made their calf gold? So they wouldn't eat it when they got hungry. See how much their "god" meant to them. Moses freed his tribe from the rule of the Pharaoh. But they said, under the Pharaoh at least we had bread, we want to go back. You're no better than they.

You said, God is not outside of you, look within so you don't idol worship. You can speak with God from inside your heart. If people had seen Jesus, Moses and Mohammad (peace be upon them all) inside their hearts before accepting what they said, things wouldn't be such a mess. You said, people celebrate Christmas, Hanukkah, and so on. Have they seen Christ in their hearts? Moslems keep going around the Ka'ba in Mecca saying they're worshipping the House of God. At the end of the lengthy ceremonies they slaughter a lamb to represent the lofty rank they've attained. First, find God, know God, then let Him slaughter your "animal self," then circumambulate His House. You said, people imitate what the Prophets did, they do not understand that the Prophets' outward actions represented a reality they were stabilized in. It doesn't take a genius to see how the Knowledge of the Almighty God has been smeared with ignorance. People are drowning in rituals!

You said, haven't you seen how that frail sprout collects all of its will and pushes through the harsh soil in order to live on a different plane? Have you even thought how that's possible? Are you less than that sprout? Instead of going through the necessary growth process you engage in hoarding, selfishness, self-praise and so on.

You said, the seed needed fertile ground and other suitable conditions to grow roots. The sprout needed the root's perseverance and toil—to move deep into the ground and gather sustenance— so it could move out of the ground. The root's faith in its destiny is so firm that it doesn't let any obstacles stand in its way; it moves around stones so it can collect the nourishment upon which its next phase of life depends! Don't you see, the sprout represents the root's belief that it can overcome the darkness. The gardener couldn't make the sprout push out of the ground. Once it's out of the ground the gardener can provide the most conducive conditions so its growth process can reach its ultimate fruition. The completion of its stages of growth represents its conviction and faith. Now evaluate yourselves!

You said, the "Trust" that God has spoken of in the Holy Book doesn't mean that something has been given to you and now you must return it. That "Trust" is the love and devotion that has been given to you which you don't value. The "Trust" God gave to the sky and the mountains, and they didn't accept it, but man accepted it because of his foolishness; he didn't know what he was accepting. I have given you so many teachings and so much knowledge, and what have you done with it? You are like the donkey who carries melons and is totally unaware of what he is carrying—knows nothing of the taste or fragrance of the melon—but just bears the load. The entire being of an amoeba becomes a mouth when it's hungry, a hand when it needs something, it breathes when it has the need, and doesn't need all the sophisticated machinery of the human being.

You said, human beings are so estranged from themselves, that if they see themselves in a mirror they won't recognize themselves. Agha Jan, is that why most people don't recognize You when they see You?

You said, perhaps it's God's compassion when pain comes your way, so you may turn to Him and forget the world that gives you the pain.

You said, 12 years ago, when You were in Your Beloved Father's Presence, it was around three or four in the morning and You hadn't slept or eaten for a few days. After days of continuous meditation, Your Father turned towards You and said, "Ask me for something, whatever You want You shall have." You responded, "There's nothing I want." You said, You had never asked Him for anything. He said, "Speak." You said, "What shall I do with this tribe?" He said, "Tell the truth, so those who are unhappy with You will leave."

You said, when raindrops fall they can fall in the ocean, the river, the brook, the pond, the earth or sand. Water returns to water and there the sun turns it to mist and it returns to the sky. But have you thought of the rain that is absorbed deep in the sand? Agha Jan, we knew immediately what this example meant.

Agha Jan, I worship and adore You. You are my Sun. I love the ground upon which Your Steps touch. When Your Love oozes in my heart, my body feels but a speck of dust next to this expansion. Then I become forlorn, for I cannot be contained and the pain of separation brings me back to earth. I begin to wish and wish, what can I be so I can be by You forever and ever. Once I wished to have the longest eyelashes in the world, then I would spread them wide underneath Your Feet, so when You take Your place on the Throne, they would cushion Your Feet from the cold marble floor. If my lashes were like the peacock's tail, how magnificent they'd look underneath Your elegant Feet.

Agha Jan, is there anything wrong with such fantasy? Once You said, it is the thought of a thing that brings you to it. So, I'll keep on thinking and thinking. Maybe the day will come when I'll always be with You—not even one instant of separation! I must not shy away from the pain of purification. How else can I dissolve in You, if not totally pure? You've said everything returns to its Origin. I keep this promise in my eyes, in my heart, and simply wait.

Agha Jan, I recall the words of the woman Saint—Rabi'a—of many centuries ago, who said, "Lord, if I worship You in fear of hell, then burn me in hell, if I worship You for the promise of paradise, then deny me paradise, but if I worship You for You, don't deny me Your Beauteous Face." Agha Jan, she must have taken these words right out of my heart. But all Your children throughout time must have said the same.

Agha Jan, I realized something today. If You fill my heart with love all the time, I could never endure the separation. So I understood why at times You veil Your love. Those are the times I feel I've done something wrong. But I always recall Your words, don't seek water, seek thirst. It was difficult for me to understand this. Yesterday after evening prayers, You suddenly revealed its meaning. Of course, what is the use of seeking the ocean when we only have a tiny cup to fill. But if we seek thirst, then the capacity expands and when You pour Your love it won't overflow. O' how I want to love You more and more and more! Agha Jan, Agha Jan, every speck of my body is vibrating with love, but it still isn't enough. You once said, there must be an element of the amber in the straw for the straw to be drawn to the amber. So that which is within this body and is drawn to You, is then You. So everything does return to its Origin. How difficult it would be for the essence to find You, see You and become one with You without this body. So, You hide Yourself in our hearts. Those who are not completely drowned in earthly desires feel the pull and move towards it, until they're faced with You. So, this is the very first resurrection, when the "I" is sparked with life in the tomb of the body—when it beholds Your Face. You said, the second resurrection is when you become stable and firm and your entire being reflects the eternity you've discovered within; for now you're truly "alive" and will never die. Agha Jan, is this the meaning of Your Beloved Father's words, "'I' is that divine inspiration of God's spirit breathed into Adam, making him alive. This inspiration of the spirit did not take place once in the beginning without a beginning, but continues without ceasing, making the tomb of the body alive so that 'selves' can survive in a divine state. Otherwise, human lives would be like the cellular annihilating lives of animals."

So, the first resurrection is when we make every effort night and day to listen to the inner call, to be guided to You, and the second resurrection is when You've cleansed us of all earthly attributes and imbued us with Your everlasting, eternal Breath. It is said in the Holy Book, "So God brings the dead out of life, and the living from the dead."

Agha Jan, I love Your subtleties. Well, after all, one of Your Names is "the Subtle." O' Agha Jan, the vapor from my laments leaves such an intoxicating trail that everyone is drawn to me. I keep telling them that it's Your love and not me. Every atom in my being is spinning. I wish I was in private so I could engage in my dance of ecstasy. But for now the airplane is not the place. I must not let out what's going on. And people think that "the whirling dance" is something they can learn its steps. They don't know that every speck of their body has to be set in motion from the love You pour their way. It's the fire of love that sparks the dance of veneration and ecstasy. I wish I could open a window and step out of the plane and simply revolve and revolve in mid-air. Agha Jan, You know I'm in no place to budge even a finger. Why are You pouring all this love my way? Is this a lesson in self-control?

I'm not complaining. I'm adoring every bit of it and can take more and more. But the plane may start spinning if You give me more. Sometimes during our Sunday services, the whirlwinds take over from within my heart. I have to exert such control so others don't see what's going on—You know there are newcomers at times, and they may wonder who's this silly child circumambulating Your House while sitting down.

Agha Jan, my soul and my heart circumambulate Your House day and night, hoping to get a glimpse of Your Face so dear. Now months have gone by and there's not a sign. I should not complain now that I'm so love-filled, since You may take away Your love and winter will set in. I rejoice and I love this state. I have hope that it's now the time of harvest after a long winter year.

Agha Jan, the picture humans paint of hell in their minds... is that the reflection of what goes on inside? I often wonder how You see us with Your all-seeing Eyes. I was thinking the other night how selfish it is of us to want to be around You. How can we put You through such an ordeal. But again, how can we become purified without Your penetrating gaze?

Agha Jan, the new sibling who comes and brings Your teachings has really worked hard. One of the siblings asked him what happens if she misses one of the daily prayers. He reflected for a moment and then said, do you want to know the truth? She said, of course. But I think after he answered her, she was sorry she'd asked. He said, 20 years ago Your Beloved Father took him under His care. He never missed a prayer, a fast, an assignment. One night he fell asleep and missed his midnight vigil. The next day at the gathering, Your Beloved Father singled him out by name and said, "For every midnight vigil you miss scratch off one year of faithful devotion." I don't think he's ever missed another one. Agha Jan, all the siblings really liked him a lot.

Agha Jan, did You look at me for five entire minutes to redeem me from all the midnight vigils I've missed? I've only missed at times of severe illness, or when winter frost blocks my heart, or when I miss Your love. But no one can ever beat me at intention. I guess if I go by what Your Beloved Father has said, even the long life of Noah would not be sufficient for the vigils I've missed. I know from tonight I'll never miss another one.

Agha Jan, I'm flying high tonight after that torment another sibling sent through me. I felt I'd been buried alive! How could I possibly live without You? What meaning could anything have without You? Never ever to see You again? Not even to hear Your voice for one second ever again? He said, get on the plane and quickly come. If you don't, there's no telling if there'll be a tomorrow, for Agha Jan has decided to leave the human race to themselves, and He's going into seclusion forever and ever, and no one is to know where He will be from now on.

I wrote You a letter, asking You permission to come and see You, begging and begging You to take me with You. So many thoughts passed through my mind. I was hysterical. I said, but I've tried to live up to my pact with Agha Jan, how can He desert me? Agha Jan, may Your blessings be with the oldest sibling. I called and asked if he would intercede for me and ask permission for me to come and see You. The way I was choking from tears alerted him that something was amiss. Please bless him, Agha Jan. He comforted me immediately and said, do you consider yourself as one of the general public? I said I hope I'm not. It's so difficult to know the right response to such questions. There's no telling what the right answer may be. He said, the matter is not the way it seems to be. His voice was comforting, but said, what's happened to your faith?

Agha Jan, there was nothing else I could ask for after that. Thank You for the gift. What a jolt that other sibling gave me. It's a good thing I have a sound heart. But I thought about it after I had recovered and was even thankful to him. The shock put all things in perspective for me. He was so dramatic. He said everyone is wearing black and mourning; it's the true month of Moharam. I said to myself, he must not know the real meaning of Moharam.

Agha Jan, the beautiful month of Moharam is here—the month of proximity, of closeness. It's the first month of the lunar year. The Shi'a think it's the month of mourning, the fundamentalists flagellate themselves, thinking they're giving alms for what went on in Karbala centuries ago. Little do they know that the Beloved Imam Hossein is the Sultan of Love; that when He was martyred the desert bloomed with the most vibrant scarlet poppies, bearing testimony to the love surging in His blood. How can they know that it was love for His Beloved that moved Him on? Agha Jan, it is now Moharam, and Your children seek the same martyrdom of the "self," to attain the closeness that this month represents. It's only Love this closeness bestows.

You've answered my prayer and I'm to be in Your Presence again. Everyone was assembled in the silence of sadness. You walked in and did not look at us. One of the siblings proceeded with the services. Not one time did You look up. When he had finished You said, when you speak, try to speak without error. I'm not going to be here to correct you from now on. So, when you speak incorrectly, it will all add up and you'll be the one at risk. The audience doesn't hear whatever you say anyway.

You said, the researcher works in balance and he is closest to the truth, that is, if he doesn't allow social and cultural filters to bias his research. The philosopher works in his imagination and that's why the common people feel closer to him. And the common people who are the majority, no matter what they hear, they still live in their superstitions and go about their foolishness—lighting candles, giving alms and so on and so forth at a nearby church, mosque, temple, etc.

You said, it's only the Prophet and the Aref who are submerged in the very core of Existence.

Your last sentence was, **The essence of all things is God.**

Agha Jan, I don't know why I recall this saying about the Blessed Amir-al-Moemenin, the Lord of believers. It is said that He never let anyone know whatever He did for anyone. There used to be a widow who had no provisions for herself and her children, and she was too meek to seek alms from strangers. One night, she sat and spoke with the Almighty God and said, Lord, don't let me ask anything from anyone but You. Help me and my small fatherless children. The next day, she found food by her door... and the next day, and the next. And this went on for years. She always said, this is the Almighty One's unseen Hand at work. That is true, but if she only knew that she could see the Almighty One's Hand at work. Agha Jan, I always want everyone to know that it's You who is the Doer of all things, how You answer the call of the sick and needy. I become so impatient when You motion me not to say anything!

Agha Jan, the flood surges from the pit of my stomach if I allow myself to think that I'll never see You again. Your posture was such that we weren't allowed to lift our eyes. But I had detected Your pain as You entered. Once I looked at Your Face and saw how deep were the lines of pain. A tear started to roll from the corner of my eye and that's when You lifted Your Eyes. I didn't look up again, but towards the end I suddenly felt an immense ball of energy set my abdomen afire. Its warmth penetrated and settled inside. I wondered later what this blessing would bring. Was it a cure to prevent an illness, was it to comfort and warm me in the coming days? To this day, I don't know why it was sent.

So, now I live with Your words and look at nature and how it speaks of the one and only Law—*la-elaha-ella-Allah*. I see flowers push out from their central core to release their soul. Earthquakes burst out from the Earth's core. All things open from their core, so they can break through their limited boundaries. I look at the lustrous pearl—the oyster's fruit of patience, perseverance, solitude and toil. When fruits are ripe they fall off the trees, but until then, they try to stay attached. Often I've gently peeled the skin of seeds and looked for the node from which their life's journey begins, there's so much tenderness underneath the skin. Why is it that humans refuse to accept that they too must find the source of their life in their own core and nourish from it until they're ripe, so they too can be set free?

The gardener sprays pesticides to protect the crops. Is there a time on our journey that You engulf us with an energy which keeps people away from us, so we don't slip and fall?

Agha Jan, everything is branded by You. How can I look at anything and not see You? Yes, they are Your manifestations, but they are not You. You are the Absolute—Absolute Perfection. And so, like the stream that flows from the highest peak of the mountain and brings forth life, all things must be Your reflection, for You are their life.

Agha Jan, the skin of most fruits and vegetables is said to have the most nutrients. Is it because the skin has the most exposure to the sun? Everything pushes out to be under the sun. The roots of the orchid don't even stay underground.

Agha Jan, why are leaves, petals and seeds heart-shaped? Is it Your love they herald and shout? If they are not heart-shaped then they spell out Your name. O' how much You've taught me. I remember when I was about six or seven years of age, all I would draw were crimson tulips and a profile ... now I know that profile was You and the crimson tulip must have been me. Everything speaks of You from behind nature's colorful veil.

Agha Jan, humans have invented so many forms of light, so we don't remain in darkness when the earth's face is turned away from the sun. Isn't it logical to think that when the day's toil is over and the sun has set, it is time to rest and go within and tend to the Sun that nourishes the soul, so we can reap the harvest from the journey's toil? When humans close their eyes and see it's dark inside, why don't they look for the light inside?

O' Agha Jan, Agha Jan, my sadness cannot be contained, for I have no shame left, I have nothing left. Are You to leave us, the Sun of our souls?

Agha Jan, I've leafed through many volumes of the books of the Great Masters, looking for the secret of their success. They all say, it's their total, unconditional love for the Almighty God, and that must be God-given for sure. Agha Jan, will You show us how to love You in the same way?

Agha Jan, why are simple words from You so devastating to me? You sent Your message, "Tell her to re-evaluate her behavior towards... she is not aware of her actions." Tonight is exactly one week from Your first reprimand, and Thursday night will be a week from the second one. I was shattered. Does innocence mean anything, Agha Jan?

Is this the story of the oyster and the pearl?

Is this total destruction the ultimate test for freedom, or are You preparing me for the separation? I'm too weak to think.

Now I must shift and do something else. I've accepted that too. Whatever it is, it is Your will done. I have no prayers, I have no supplication, I accept whatever is Your will. I have no remorse, for I've done my very best.

Will it mean anything if I say, I can hear my hair grow white from pain?

I no longer fear that one day You may let go. I am experiencing it and accepting it. You once said, isn't it the will of the sun for the earth to revolve and revolve around the sun? I've always kept quiet, never complained about others. Always saying, it's okay, Agha Jan knows. I still know that You know. It is Your will, love cannot be forced. I've accepted that and I am at peace now.

There is nothing I want of the world. There's nothing in the world that tempts me. Nothing creates the slightest motion of desire within me. I don't need fulfillment from anything outside. You've taught me so much. I only have one question and this too seems to be dimming away. Where did I go wrong that You slowly put me aside?

You are God, and what can I say in front of the All-Knowing, the All-Seeing? It all seems like a dream. The word God no longer seems to set anything in motion. I still have faith and worship You and know whatever You do must be done. What significance can an itsy bitsy tiny little thing like me have in front of God's great master plan?

I'm silent now...words, words, I have no more. I've visited with God for 11 full years. I've said more than any ear could have ever expected to hear. And so much I've left unsaid. But I must say this, if there is anyone who is truly searching for God, keep searching, for God does answer. No one but Him knows why He answers, and what will happen after that. There is just one very important thing, don't ever ask God for anything. Leave everything to Him!

Yes, I close my heart, my door, my soul. I am completely empty, empty of the world, empty of desires, empty of all—a difficult state to describe. Perhaps it's like someone who has lost the perfect beloved, and nothing but memories can have luster on a now empty page. It is neither emptiness nor sadness, but a feeling I cannot describe. So a seed was planted and it bloomed and bloomed so very fast, only because the gardener had his watchful eye on it all the time. By the same token it wilted before the other flowers began their bloom.

This roller coaster is unreal, Agha Jan. That same sibling called me and said, Agha Jan's coming, arrange your travel plans. Of course I was happy, but I was also sad. I didn't know what to expect. Would I be able to cover the bruise? Would it be healed in such a few days? But I was totally resigned to whatever was to happen.

I beheld Your Face, You walked in and everyone bowed. You looked at me. We were told to come in. I walked in and You asked, how are you? I said, thanks is to God. We sat around You. Then You walked and glanced at everything—the inspection of all things and everyone with just one glance. Such elegance! It's autumn now. Last year You came in summer, the year before in spring, and the year before that in winter. I wonder if the harvest is to Your liking? There were siblings there who hadn't hatched, there were real tiny ones. I was the oldest. I was given a seat very close to You and of course had the privilege of being passed blessed food from You. I ate and ate, all of it for health. I was not full, but thought I should not overdo it either. Not even once did I lift up my head. Lunch was over as they began to clear away the dishes and the food. I got up to go and sit by the wall. Very gently I passed by You. As I was about to sit, You said, I've given directions on the notes you've sent. I thanked You. Then You said, ask, concerning the itemized letter you sent Me. Then You added, but don't ask Me. Agha Jan, I've learned that the time has passed when I could ask You questions, or expect any answers. Agha Jan, You've even veiled Yourself from my dreams. It had been eight months since You'd spoken to me. As I looked up You sent the loveliest purple-lavender orchid flying my way, saying something about my temperament. I only caught the last part. Then You said with the most beautiful smile, will your temperament ever improve? I held my orchid in the palm of my vibrating hands, my vision became blurred. What could this mean, receiving a flower in such a way directly from God's Perfect Hand?

As I sat with my orchid well placed in my heart, and my head bent down, inhaling with all my being the smoke coming from Your pipe and absorbing the peace that filled the room—boundaries faded. A rustle close by made me aware that I hadn't been there for a very long time. I wasn't aware that everyone had moved away and sat in a circle a few feet away from You. I thought I too must move. As I got up to take my place next to the others, You looked at me. I knew that I shouldn't have moved just because the others had moved, for it is You who must direct the moves.

Everything seemed to be moving smoothly that day. You answered so many questions that the siblings had. You asked the physicist if he had found anything reproachful in what You had said the night before. He said, how can anything be amiss when it's God who speaks. You said, why do you look at Me? God is God and I am Me. Agha Jan, You always hide Your identity. He then asked You what is the way to succeed on the path to God. You said, have you ever gone mountain climbing? He said, yes. You said, I don't mean climbing hills. He said, I guess I haven't then. You said, what do you need to go mountain climbing? He started enumerating, then added, the desire to go is needed as well. You said, if the desire isn't there you wouldn't even prepare. You said, do you ever look behind you when you're climbing high? He said yes. You said, it shows you haven't climbed a mountain yet. You said, if you look down, you're sure to fall. The path of God is the same. When you've turned your face towards God—and that's repentance, I've often said—then if you turn your face away and look back, you'll have a bad fall. If you continue climbing, midway you may get tired and the path may seem longer than it really is, but that's only because you've gotten tired now. The path that's left to be tread is the same length. You need enthusiasm and love to give you fuel to move on and not stop.

Another sibling asked, why is the path to God so difficult? You said, it's the path of the world that's tough—you always worry about your job, payments, illness, and so on, but the path to God only requires an earnest and susceptible heart. Then You changed Your pace and tone and said, do you remember weddings in the old land? You seem to be older than I so you must remember. You said, the tradition called for all the wedding things to be carried on large elaborate trays on people's heads from street to street until they reached the wedding house. Now if someone was smart he'd go and just hold up the corner of a tray as everyone proceeded towards the bridal place. No one checks I.D.'s at times as these, everyone's festive, whoever comes in receives his tip. You said, be smart, now that the door's open, just walk in. Then she said, what shall I do, it seems my daily prayers seem to get me nowhere! You said, in any undertaking you need preparation, if you don't start will the rest get done? You can't go to the university if you haven't completed all the studies of the previous years. So be patient. Then You said, when you invite a guest do you expect your guest to come, or was it just formality when the offer was made?

Another sibling asked You, what is the way to start on the path of God? You said, what do you need when you go to grade one? All you need is a clean notebook and a pencil in hand, then the teacher will write the assignment on the first line and you'll follow his hand. Agha Jan, in these two statements you gave her the blessings for a lifetime of devotion and prayer.

Another one asked You, how can we know God, we don't know Him. You said, whenever you become free of yourself and of others then you will know God.

Another sibling who had been busy with the preparations and had missed Your answers asked, how can we go on the Path? You said, the cloth that you spread on the floor for lunch to be served on has two sides. The side which was folded in was the side upon which lunch was served. The other side faced the carpet. But when you cleared away the things and began to fold the cloth back in place you had its wrong face in place. Do you know the significance of this? The side facing the carpet is not clean for healthy food to be placed over it. When you eat do you eat for health or do you want contaminants to ruin your health? Until when are you going to keep this side of your heart mingled with dirt? Keep your heart clean, so the food God gives you for health won't be contaminated!

Agha Jan, then a very new sibling who hadn't hatched yet asked with much apology if he could ask You a question on someone else's request. Permission was granted. He said, this friend of his wanted to know about this thing that he heard called journey to a realm known as "white brotherhood." He said, it is said that while the soul travels there another soul comes and inhabits the body. When he wants to return, his protective shield is hurt. What must he do? You said, this statement has many problems with it from the start. You said, "white brotherhood" and similar things are all political cults used to deceive people, they have nothing to do with the journey of the soul. You said, when you go on a trip and come back, does your house have the same familiarity and feeling for you as when you were leaving it? Or did it take you awhile to adjust and have the same feelings as before? The house hadn't changed, but it was you who'd had intervening experiences and had to adjust. You said, consider a car. You and your friend have two different cars. If you want to drive his car is it as easy as driving your own car at the start? So you say, this soul goes somewhere and another soul comes in his body. What happens in the interval when one leaves and the other comes? Is the body lifeless? Then You picked up the pitcher of water in Your right Hand and the glass in Your left. You poured all the water into the glass and then said, what about this water that stuck to the pitcher's walls, what about it? Then You said, this entire system has adapted itself to the commands of its first inhabitant, how will the second soul handle it? Just suppose that I give you My shoes to wear for a month. When you return My shoes, will they feel the same on My Feet as when I gave them to you? You said, suppose that he did establish communication with other spirits, so what? What is the ultimate result of that? People communicate here and what becomes of it? He said, these weren't my questions, but my friend wanted to know. Then You said with much tenderness, isn't it better to ask your own questions so you will grow? Then he posed his own question, and You began with the most gentle and firm manner to teach him.

Agha Jan, tears swelled up in my eyes as I recalled those days gone past. Memories, my precious memories.

Then the most common question was asked: How can we rest from the clutch of the self? You said, to go on this path requires love, enthusiasm, harmony and oneness of origin. Does someone who is in love notice anything else, does he bother with anything?

A young man asked, how can we develop the capacity for learning? You said, if you go to a gynecologist will he give you any advice? He may just tell you something so you don't feel out of place, but it is evident that you don't belong there.

I don't remember the next question that was posed, but I know You said, if a child that is born has not developed the necessary tools (arms, limbs, organs, etc.) for his survival on earth, will he be able to develop them here? When the fetus is in the womb does he call for a doctor to tend to it? Or, the doctor comes when the need is there? Look at God's mysterious ways, whenever there's a need the answer's right next to it. When a child is born and cries in hunger, the mother's breasts swell up with milk to respond to his urgent need. Whenever there is a true need, be sure that it will be answered. Sit and speak with God in earnest, for God hears and answers.

You stood up and everyone got up. You said, take a few minutes, freshen up and rest, we have the evening ahead. I was still in a daze holding my orchid with care. Slowly the guests began to arrive. The sibling in charge gave me the best seat in the House. We sat in meditation for an hour. Before anyone got up I saw You in my heart and so I got up and there You were, Agha Jan.

After the chanting and offerings of prayers, the Holy Book was read and You turned a new leaf in the book of our souls.

You said, Islam means freedom. The human being has different dimensions. His cellular level is attached to the earth due to its composition. The other dimension brings news from the very core of nature, and the ultimate dimension is that which the Almighty has said, "I created man in My own image." The function of religion is to train humans to attain this state. As long as you are absorbed in your cellular level, you have no knowledge of your true rank as designated by God. As long as you use your senses only to satisfy your needs, you'll never know their infinite capacity. Prophets are those who have discovered their infinite capacity; they have attained the state of receiving revelation, and by revelation I do not mean you have to go from somewhere to somewhere else. If you look closely at a light bulb that's lit, you'll see that the light expands from it and illuminates the room. Revelation is the same expansion, where God manifests in cellular form. That's what's meant by what people commonly say, "The Holy Book has descended." Can you also give your self the same rank?

You said, humans bear all the genetic and mental states of all of their forefathers ever since life existed. Just look how much you bear with you. People say this child is born with jaundice, they don't see that the blueprint for this was laid two generations ago when someone was an opium addict or drank heavily or used spices excessively. They just see the illness that has now manifest. Or, you see someone with deformities in their skin, they don't go back to see that someone was down with syphilis or such things. Anyway, you carry all the loads of all those who preceded you; now, with all this inheritance, how much true health do you have that you want to mend other people's ways? People form groups and say we want to bring about social justice and so on. First heal yourself, find the remedy, then help others.

You said, this life is like a crossroad through which everyone must pass. Some become acquainted and feel comfortable with each other so they journey on together. But should their paths separate, then they'll never meet again. Agha Jan, this statement brought to my mind the pact I made with You 11 years ago.

You said, you've come from the **source of life**, and to it you must return. The body is the tool given to you to make the return possible.

Just look around you, every piece of machinery has its own specific function, and these are man-made. Don't sell yourself short!

You said, there isn't a being who doesn't need God, ultimately all beings end up needing God. How often have you called God to serve you? How many times has He answered. If he doesn't answer once then you start cursing. It doesn't matter, God is compassionate, He is telling you that you are cursing yourself.

You said, whatever seed you plant, that's what you'll harvest in its own time. If you plant the seed of greed, jealousy, envy, that's what you'll have at the time of harvest. If you plant the seed of love, that's what you'll have. Try it, it's autumn now. The soil is ready and many seeds are blown into it and they'll grow roots. Even if you plant a good seed, all these weeds will strangle it. But see how all the energy of the soil is used for the harvest of weeds. Look inside yourself and see how you want to use all the energy and capacity that has been given to you.

You said, unless that seed sprouts up and bears fruit, and that fruit ripens to its full capacity, it will not have fulfilled its mission. Look at the five daily prayers. The night prayer is when the seed is growing roots; the morning prayer is when the sprout pushes out of the darkness of the earth; the noon and afternoon prayers represent its growth and blossoming; and the dusk prayer is when the perfect fragrant fruit is presented. At this time the tree says, "I am alive and I have fulfilled my mission– I am as I was made to be."

You said, water is the agent that brings things to their delicate state. Look how water transfers all that the plant needs to create such delicate petals. What similarity has the root to the petal? Jesus manifested that ultimate sublime state, can you claim that you are a Christian?

You said, whatever you see in someone else it means you have it yourself. Someone who doesn't have the capacity of taste, can he describe what sour tastes like?

You said, what is your wish of this infinite Existence? Just to do the same basic functions as animals? That's fine. But I tell you, that's not why you were created. If you don't think you're worth more it doesn't mean you're not. In whatever state you are, that's how much you'll get of what existence has to offer. If you don't see behind these walls it doesn't mean nothing exists behind them. Seeing is other than the breaking of light which registers things in the brain. The arm has cells, muscles, nerves, etc., but it doesn't see. It wasn't meant to see. The eyes were made with that function in mind. Now consider if someone who can converge all of vision's capacity at one point gets behind that lens, how much more can the eye see?

How much of the capacity of the solar plexus are you using? The bare minimum for the digestive system and such things. Its name should tell you that it's connected to the sun. Total concentration in the solar plexus will give you all the knowledge of the sun. The same holds true for all the other systems. So, know yourself before it's too late.

The Holy Book was recited and we began to chant. My eyes were closed and when I opened them You were gone. I knew You'd be leaving before the evening would end. Somehow something's changed. I've resigned to whatever is at hand. The halo of sadness surrounds my heart. I know deep down what is to evolve.

Just a week later we were told we would be in Your Presence for the Holy Day, the 17th of November.

So much happened in these three weeks. How painful and how sad. I tried to obey all of Your directions with all my heart, but so much intervened—so much pain, so much hurt, so much, so much....

You know what happened on that Blessed Day, I don't have the heart to repeat it at all. I was unsettled. I could not chant, I could not focus on the words. The supplications and prayers had no meaning for me. I had no tears. Agha Jan, You spoke with patience, You spoke with kindness, You spoke with compassion, You spoke with concern. You spoke as a father who is about to leave his children for a very long time. You gave us much more than we will ever know. Once You stopped and said, don't try to analyze what is being said, function as a tape recorder and simply record, so when the time comes you'll have the words available. You said, learn to leave your social conditioning behind, allow the brain to function without static and interruption from all your inputs. Agha Jan, I have understood that the most important thing is to be fully present so we can take away with us all the blessings that the words enfold... especially on such an unusual day.

Agha Jan, before Your Beloved Father's tape was played You said, Your Beloved Father had spoken these words 25 years ago. You said, listen carefully to what you'll hear, perhaps for you it will be a learning experience and for Me a punishment. My soul seemed to know Your Beloved Father's words so well. How He spoke of You! His gentleness and love for humanity was painful to my heart, because all the while I saw You. He told us never to be proud and arrogant, but to serve everyone with an open and sincere heart. He said, be kind to each other and to everyone else. He said, don't lie to yourselves and don't lie to God. He said, this is the path of love, of service, of lowliness. He said, You are the heart of Your Beloved Grandfather, and He is revered as the Lord of Love and Knowledge, and how it is His wish that the Knowledge be entrusted to You, so You can bring this message to mankind. How He praised You, Agha Jan! How my heart and soul knew His words. He said, Your entire life had been spent in the service of God, not a trace of anything but God could be seen in You.

Agha Jan, there was a moment's silence, and I recalled Your Beloved Great Grandfather's words in His Holy Book:

> *That I attain this elevated rank, this dignity at par—*
> *is but a reflection in the fountain of love's nectar*
> *springing forth from Your divine grace*
> *as away from all else I turn my face!*
> *Riding upon annihilation's fine state, I found the profound*
> *Truth: The very existence is existent from*
> *Your love unbound!*
> *Even this submission, this capacity of acceptance*
> *is but Your boon; my vow's confirmation*
> *a sign of Your Presence.*

As Your Beloved Father spoke, I saw the lines of pain and sadness deepen on Your Face. How You must endure the separation from Your Beloved. How painful it must be. I wished that Your pain would be mine. My only prayer was to You and for You. How You must suffer for our ignorance, how You must suffer for being among us. Forgive us, Thou Generous One.

I knew this was to be the day. At the very end You said, I've planted the seed and it has sprouted. Now it's all in your hands, let's see what you'll have at the time of harvest. You said, each location now has it's responsible head, refer all your needs to them. I don't think you'll see me in such gatherings again. Agha Jan, can a sprout bloom without the sun?

Agha Jan, Agha Jan, the nights are getting longer and darker, has the earth ceased to revolve around the sun?

Agha Jan, I have one very special memory. One day in between interviews, You took me to a nearby museum and walked me through it. You taught me why a work is great, why one is weak, why another is always remembered. One sentence which I always remember is this, Look at this painting, one can tell that the painter has truly put himself into it. Many people paint sceneries, they look nice, but this is different, the artist can be seen in it. Agha Jan, Agha Jan, I see You in everything, in all things. Memories, memories.... You walked me through the building, through the elevator, all with such elegance. You walked me through the traffic so carefully. There was a ticket on my windshield. As it occurred to me that I'd forgotten to put money in the meter, You said, this is an example for you to remember, how people blame God for their own negligence. Every instant is a learning experience in Your Presence, Agha Jan. My precious, precious memories...

Agha Jan, once I asked You if fairy tales were true. You said, they are true experiences of the Masters told in symbols, but through time people lost touch, and they became simple tales.

Agha Jan, I want to tell you a tale so very close to my heart. There was once a very innocent little tiny chick who knew no one and followed no one but her mother. The mother had many chicks to tend to. When all the other chicks played, ate, slept, squabbled, our tiny little chick always kept her eye on mother, always looking at mother, always concerned about mother. One day mother told them that she'll have to go away and tend to other matters. So, she appointed a few of the older siblings to look after the rest. Mother would send all messages through them. The oldest sibling remembered mother had said, "A long cold winter I see ahead." So, he said to himself, "I wonder if this is mother's ultimate test of faith? I wonder how everyone's going to fare?" Our tiny chick who'd never mingled with the rest, or learned their tricks and habits, was scrutinized and blamed for lack of respect. They took their complaints to mother about her neglects. They didn't tell mother it was their ego at stake. Mother sent her verdict, "Tell her to obey and respect the elders." Our chick sulked but obeyed. A lump began to grow in her throat, she missed mother so. The more she obeyed the more forceful they became and the lump in her throat got bigger and bigger each day. She was all alone, she missed mother so. The elders had no mercy on our little tiny chick. They didn't give her a moment's rest or peace. They made sure she knew that it was they who now ruled, and towards them her face must now be turned. So, from all sides she was pressed, beaten and bruised, and the lump in her throat became too big for her frail body to endure. One day, as I was walking on the path on my way home, I found our little chick by the roadside. Her tiny head was resting on a smooth black stone, her wings had fallen by her side, and the lump in her throat had oozed out into a gold crystalline tear drop reflecting the black stone.

I slowly bent down and touched her tiny head with a gentle kiss. I whispered in her ear, whenever it's cloudy and bleak down here I get on a plane and move on up there, the sun's always out when you ride above the clouds. She didn't budge. She didn't move. Her eyes remained closed. I could see from her frail limbs she had ceased to ride

on the wings of hope some time ago. I saw a shadow settle over her face
and I heard her humming a song. I moved closer to listen, the closer I
got the fainter her voice got.

Then I recalled her face and began to hum to myself,

> O' Madonna of Seville,
> O' Madonna
> Is this why
> Your tears are
> pearls,
> sapphires and
> ruby-fire?
> O' Madonna, Madonna,
> How you loved and loved....

Agha Jan, who misses the laments of the nightingale, but the rose?
And who misses the fragrance of the rose?

Agha Jan, will You always keep me in Your Garden of Paradise?

In God's Great Name

The crimson melody from my falling tears,
Settles as lustrous rubies at Thy majestic Feet.

Thy presence transforms mud into heavenly musk,

Thy voice breaks the heart's winter ice into
Tears of joy.

Thy remembrance shatters the silent solitude,
My winter eyes bloom when I recall,

Thy stature, Thy poise, Thy elegance,
Thy perfection unparalleled.

O' Perfect One, thou Eternal,
Thou, illuminating Sun,

Thou,
Horizons of glistening moonlight,
Bewitching eras of Psalms,
Humming clamor of expectant eyes,
Pulse of an awakening seed,
Vast expanse of the skies,
Heavenly nocturnal bond,

Roses trimmed by Thy elegant touch,
Grow to blooming fragrance by Thy patient Eyes.

My earnest cry,
Is to Thee,

Thou, who sets afire the blazing sun,
Thy Palm, the heavenly throne of orbiting stars,

Thou,
Promised Paradise.

University Press of America,® Inc.
4720 Boston Way
Lanham, Maryland 20706

12 Hid's Copse Rd.
Cummor Hill, Oxford OX2 9JJ

Library of Congress Cataloging-in-Publication Data

Shashaani, Avideh.
Promised Paradise : Agha Jan-Sufism's Secret Divulged / Avideh
Shashaani.
p.   cm.
l. Sufi poetry. I. Title.
BP187.7.M28S5   1993   297'.43--dc20   93-28463 CIP

ISBN 0-8191-9254-6 (cloth alk. ppr.)
ISBN 0-8191-9255-4 (pbk: alk. ppr.)

First Printing, 1993
Second Printing, 1997

Cover design, artwork, typography by:
Cynthia Comitz
Cover photography by Ping Amranand

Promised Paradise

Agha Jan — Sufism's Secret Divulged

Avideh Shashaani

UNIVERSITY
PRESS OF
AMERICA

Lanham • New York • London